D1290742

Poststructuralism and Educational Research

Poststructuralism and Educational Research

Michael A. Peters and Nicholas C. Burbules

ROWMAN & LITTLEFIELD PUBLISHERS, INC.
Lanham • Boulder • New York • Toronto • Oxford

ROWMAN & LITTLEFIELD PUBLISHERS, INC.

Published in the United States of America
by Rowman & Littlefield Publishers, Inc.
A wholly owned subsidiary of The Rowman & Littlefield Publishing Group, Inc.
4501 Forbes Boulevard, Suite 200, Lanham, Maryland 20706
www.rowmanlittlefield.com

PO Box 317, Oxford, OX2 9RU, UK

Copyright © 2004 by Rowman & Littlefield Publishers, Inc.

All rights reserved. No part of this publication may be reproduced, stored in a
retrieval system, or transmitted in any form or by any means, electronic, mechanical,
photocopying, recording, or otherwise, without the prior permission of the publisher.

British Library Cataloguing in Publication Information Available

Library of Congress Cataloging-in-Publication Data

Peters, Michael (Michael A.), 1948–
  Poststructuralism and educational research / Michael A. Peters and
Nicholas C. Burbules.
     p. cm.—(Philosophy, theory, and educational research series)
  Includes bibliographical references and index.
  ISBN 0-8476-9119-5 (cloth : alk. paper)—ISBN 0-8476-9120-9 (pbk. :
alk. paper) 1. Education—Research—Philosophy. 2. Poststructuralism. I.
Burbules, Nicholas C. II. Title. III. Series: Philosophy, theory, and
educational research.
  LB1028.P37 2004
  370'.7'201—dc22
                                                              2003019256

♾™ The paper used in this publication meets the minimum requirements of American
National Standard for Information Sciences—Permanence of Paper for Printed Library
Materials, ANSI/NISO Z39.48-1992.

We dedicate this book to all our students, past and present, who have helped us to clarify the concepts and understand the approaches of those philosophers and thinkers — in philosophy, the humanities, and education — who have come to be called "poststructuralist."

Contents

Acknowledgments

We would like to thank Tina Besley and Joyce Atkinson for their helpful comments, support, and forbearance. Our thanks also to numerous friends and colleagues in the field of education who have provided insightful work (in the real sense of the term), much of which has figured in this book: James Marshall, Zelia Gregoriou, Henry Giroux, Cleo Cherryholmes, Tina Besley, Gert Biesta, Lynda Stone, Patti Lather, Stephen Ball, Lucy Holmes, Betsan Martin, Elizabeth Grierson, Janet Mansfield, Ho-Chia Chuen, Wang Chengbing, Elizabeth St. Pierre, Wanda Pillow, Walter Humes, Bob Davis, Paul Standish, Paul Smeyers, Richard Smith, and many others. Finally, our thanks also to Dean Birkenkamp and Alison Sullenberger at Rowman & Littlefield both for their editorial support, guidance, and patience. This book has been a long time coming. We hope that it will be a useful introduction to a complex skein of thought.

Series Preface

This book with Michael Peters is the third in a series appearing with Rowman & Littlefield Publishers: "Philosophy, Theory, and Educational Research." Contemporary educational research has been experiencing an explosion of new methodologies and approaches to inquiry. Many of these approaches have drawn from philosophical or theoretical positions that underlie their determinations of research methods, aims, and criteria of validity. Yet the substance of these philosophical or theoretical assumptions is not always made clear to readers, and so it is difficult for them to judge those assumptions for themselves.

This series is designed to explore some of the dominant philosophical and theoretical positions influencing educational research today, in a manner that does justice to the substance of these views and shows their relevance for research aims and practices. Each volume shows how a particular set of philosophical and theoretical positions affects the methods and aims of educational research and discusses specific examples of research that show these orientations at work. The emphasis is on lively, accessible, and theoretically sound explorations of the issues. These books are intended to be of interest not only to educational researchers, but to anyone in education wanting to understand what these various "isms" are about.

This series features a distinguished international group of scholars. It is important for the reader to know that the first author of each volume has had primary responsibility for conceptualizing and drafting the text. The series editor has played an active role in selecting the topics and organization for each volume, has interacted regularly with the first author as the text has been drafted, and has had a relatively free hand in revising the text and adding or suggesting new material. This is more than the role that editors normally play, and so second authorship seemed the appropriate appellation. But the predominant voice and point of view for each volume in the series is the first author's. It could not be otherwise, because no coauthor could equally advocate all the positions, many of them mutually inconsistent, argued for in these volumes.

Introduction

Poststructuralism, and its implications for the movement known as "postmodernism," is a major topic of discussion in the humanities and in social theory and research, including educational research. The works of the major authors in this tradition (Michel Foucault, Jean-François Lyotard, Hélène Cixous, Jacques Derrida, Gilles Deleuze, and Donna Haraway, to name a few) are challenging and difficult. Yet more and more theorists and researchers in educational scholarship use this term to describe their work. What does "poststructuralism" mean for these authors, and what significance does it have for educational inquiry? This is the central question of the present book.

This book, exploring the impact of poststructuralism in language, intends to make the basic issues at stake clear, accessible, and relevant for a broad readership in education. We highlight the implications of a poststructuralist stance for the conception of the researcher and research subject in education, for the aims of educational research, and for forms of analysis and methods of investigation in educational research. We also describe the particular ways in which important and influential scholars (including Henry Giroux, Patti Lather, and Stephen Ball) have tried to incorporate the poststructuralist perspective into their investigations of educational issues. The emphasis throughout this book is on making these complex theoretical issues tangible, and making clear the moral and political commitments that drive this sometimes abstract intellectual movement.

While often stereotyped as inaccessible and aloof, poststructuralism actually offers many writers, among both the precursors to poststructuralism and the first generation of poststructuralist thinkers themselves, who addressed themselves directly to educational concerns. This supports, prima facie, the case for poststructuralism's direct relevance and significance to educational theory, policy, and practice. At one level, then, there is no need to try to imagine a case for the educational relevance and significance of something called "poststructuralism" by theorizing about potential *applications* of it. There is already a substantial body of work *based in educational concerns* where these writers developed their broader theoretical ideas. Let us give some brief indications of what we mean.

Education (as *bildung*, meaning "self-cultivation") played an important part in Friedrich Nietzsche and Martin Heidegger's philosophies—two frequently cited precursors to the poststructuralist movement—and both wrote explicitly on the nature of education and educational institutions. Nietzsche's essays, "Schopenhauer as Educator" and "On the Future of Our Educational Institutions," written in the 1870s while he was still a professor, provide an indication of the significance he granted to education and its role in the process of cultural renewal. Heidegger's controversial essay, "The Self-Assertion of the German University," in which he was prepared to sacrifice academic freedom in the name of national purpose, and the politically dubious statements he made when he was rector of Freiberg University during the Nazi period, should not obscure his wider contributions as one of the seminal critics of the university. His works on thinking and learning have not been (in our view) adequately considered in educational circles and the full import of his evaluation of humanism given in his famous "Letter on Humanism" has not been critically discussed by educational theorists, even although it centrally involves a model of education.

Roland Barthes (1977: 192), in his now famous essay "Writers, Intellectuals, Teachers," indicates the political stakes in teaching, which by definition has some inherently authoritarian elements. We can, as teachers, accept the authoritarian role, remain mute, nudge speech toward writing, or practice "peaceable speech," which is the option that comes closest to deconstructive teaching. Vincent Leitch discusses Roland Barthes' deconstructive pedagogy in the following lucid terms:

> Barthes' whole pedagogical project goes in the direction of deracination and desedimentation, on the one hand, and pleasure and play, on the other: uproot the frozen text; break down stereotypes and opinions; suspend or baffle the violence and authority of language; pacify or lighten oppressive paternal powers; disorient the Law; let classroom discourse float, fragment, digress; seek ascetic or libidinal abandonment of the teaching body/self. The politics here is resolutely anti-authoritarian and anarchist. (1996: 75)

Michel Foucault also developed an explicit critique of pedagogical institutions as a central part of his critique of the human sciences, and, in particular, a critique of the "disciplinary" model of the school, where the productive power of normalization and individualization is seen to be embodied in certain techniques of surveillance. Ultimately, Foucault would say that in such techniques we learn to administer to ourselves in pursuit of the goal of reproducing knowledge and reproducing ourselves as knowers. Like Derrida, described below, Foucault also took an active political role in shaping education reforms in France.

Jacques Derrida has been active in *Groupe de recherches sur l'enseignment philosophique* (Group for Research on Philosophic Teaching, GREPH) established in 1974 to halt proposed reforms that would limit and reduce the teaching of philosophy as a subject in the senior school. Gregory Ulmer countenances the suggestion made by Edward Said that Derrida has nothing but a pedagogy and that the place of pedagogy in Western thought for Derrida is a corollary of his analysis of writing:

> Everything that he says about the bias against writing in logocentrism applies as well to pedagogy, understood as a representation and communication that models itself after the Book. Teaching in the age of Hegel or the post-age, thus, has a retrospective, rather than a prospective, function, Derrida states, and operates by a semiotic logic: "Teaching delivers signs, the teaching body produces (shows and puts forth) proofs, more precisely signifiers supposing knowledge of a previous signified. Referred to this knowledge, the signifier is structurally second. Every university puts language in this position of delay or derivation in relation to meaning or truth." (Ulmer, 1985: 163)

Derrida addresses himself to the question of the modern university, asking whether the notion of reason still provides the necessary legitimation or raison d'être for the university institution in the era of technoscience. The politics of research and teaching can no longer be reduced to a problematics centered on the nation-state, but must take into account "technomilitary networks that are apparently multi- or trans-national in form" (Derrida, 1983: 11). In this context, the distinction between applied and basic research has broken down. Within postmodernity it is no longer possible to distinguish the principle of reason from the idea of technology. The military and the state, through their investments in research, can often control and even censor knowledge through "limiting the means" to support inquiry or through "regulating the support for production, transmission and diffusion" of knowledge. In addition, external forces are intervening within the university. Presses, foundations, private institutions, think-tanks and the mass media intrude in the politics of the university in a characteristically novel way. Derrida suggests that the concept of "informatization" is the "most general operator here" (1983: 14), which integrates the basic to the oriented, the purely rational to the technical.

Jean-François Lyotard (1984) perhaps most famously addresses the role and status of knowledge and education in *The Postmodern Condition*, where they have become commodified, technologized, and fallen under the sway of the logic of what he calls "performativity."

The contributions of Lyotard and others' theories to understanding education are explained and elaborated on much more thoroughly later in this book. But already two features will be clear. One is that poststructuralist theory and vocabulary are often unfamiliar and challenging, involving new coinages or rearticulations of familiar terms in new ways; poststructuralist theory can be extremely abstract, even when it is discussing a down-to-earth activity such as education. As a result, many find these works arduous to read in the primary sources—in fact, given its frequent propensity for playfulness and experimentation with language, many find it simply infuriating. Second, poststructuralist theory is committed to a critique of dominant institutions and modes of speaking, thinking, and writing—which means it is often set against what is most familiar and comfortable for us, asking us to see the danger or the harm even in what we take to be "good." These sorts of challenges can be hard to take, and sometimes seem on their face to be outrageous. For both of these reasons, poststructuralism has had difficulty making theoretical inroads, especially in education, where currency and "relevance" are often elevated over purely intellectual exploration for its own sake, and where the good intentions behind educational institutions and practices are taken for granted.

The milieu of educational research today tends to be relatively conservative, being largely state or federally funded and still strongly imbued with the positivist ethos it inherited during its historical development and professionalization as a legitimate field of study. Meanwhile, poststructuralism at its broadest level offers a philosophical attack upon the scientific pretensions of social inquiry, including a critique of the very Enlightenment norms that educational research typically prides itself on: "truth," "objectivity," and "progress." Poststructuralism provides a philosophical corrective to the confidence with which mainstream theorists allow these concepts or terms to remain unexamined and unreconstructed in face of the demise of epistemological foundationalism.

Poststructuralism, by contrast, adopts an anti- or post-epistemological standpoint, and is fiercely anti-foundationalist. It also adopts an anti-realist position, at least when it comes to questions of meaning and reference, rejecting the established picture of knowledge as an accurate representation. In particular, poststructuralism tends to eschew the traditional account of truth corresponding to reality, emphasizing the idea that language functions as a *differential system*. Poststructuralist thought also tends to emphasize anti-essentialism and historicize questions of who we are and what we are studying when we study ourselves; it questions the humanism underlying traditional accounts of the unified, autonomous, and transparent self.

Against transcendental arguments and viewpoints, poststructuralism also pits a many-sided perspectivism. From Nietzsche, poststructuralism inherits a critique of "truth" and a diagnosis and critique of many entrenched binary oppositions (e.g., mind/body, nature/culture, male/female, reason/madness, rationality/emotions) that bedevil Western metaphysics and our ways of thinking. Poststructuralism analyzes and deconstructs these binary oppositions to unmask the way they manufacture hierarchical tables of value that often arbitrarily privilege one set over others.

Politically speaking, poststructuralism aims to expose structures of domination by diagnosing "power/knowledge" relations and their manifestations in our classifications, examinations, practices, and institutions. It aims to produce an "incredulity towards metanarratives," to disassemble the structures, the "moves" and strategies of official discourse (whether the state, the party, or political movements and institutions that claim to speak for others). It aims to analyze power relations in communication and the pedagogies of modern forms of mass media.

As a general trend, poststructuralism highlights the centrality of language to human activity and culture—its materiality, its linguisticality, and its pervasive ideological nature. Poststructuralism emphasizes the self-undermining and self-deconstructing character of discourse. In this way it also calls into question the naturalness of the disciplines, stressing that disciplines are historical formations. For example, poststructuralism entertains a set of complex relations between philosophy and literature, overcoming traditional demarcations to highlight philosophy as a kind of writing and the philosophical nature of literary fictions. Above all, it provides new practices of "reading"—both texts and text analogues—and new and experimental forms of "writing." Poststructuralism as a contemporary philosophical movement offers a range of *theories* (of the text), *critiques* (of institutions), *new concepts*, and *new forms of analysis* (of power) that are, as we try to show here, highly relevant and significant for the study of education.

Chapter 1 begins with an attempt to distinguish poststructuralism from postmodernism—a concept that is related but quite distinct. One source of confusion in the literature is a tendency to conflate them. We turn next to the tradition of "structuralism," to which poststructuralism is a response, of course, and explain what its project was where poststructuralism shares that project, and where it differs from it. In the course of this overview, we touch upon important terms and ideas that will be developed later in the text, especially the key ideas of *difference*, *archaeology*, *genealogy*, and *deconstruction*.

Chapter 2 addresses the aims of poststructuralist inquiry by way of questioning the conceptions of "science" and "research" that drive most academic inquiry, including educational research. (It is typical of a poststructural approach that before it can tell you what it *is*, it needs to explain what it is *not*). This investigation traces the history of the natural and human sciences, where and why they diverged, focusing especially on the emergence of *knowledge* and *understanding* as crucial aims of research. Understanding these issues today, one must inquire into who is doing *what counts as* "science" and "research," where it is carried out, how it is funded, and how these relate to a particular political and state formation. Certainly this is true of educational research.

Chapter 3 addresses the question of "methods," although again poststructuralism wants to question the technical ways in which research "methods" often get thought of and "applied." In this sense poststructuralism does not offer methods. But in examining some of the most influential modes of analysis in poststructuralism—*archaeology*, *genealogy*, *deconstruction*, and *feminist poststructuralism*—readers will see many ways in which these approaches have supported, and can support, rigorous educational analysis and critique.

Chapter 4 provides extended discussions of scholars who have drawn from poststructuralist ideas and approaches in studying educational problems. We focus especially on three well-known figures: Henry Giroux, Patti Lather, and Stephen Ball. They are by no means monolithic in method or outlook, but they draw from the works of the major poststructuralist thinkers and add to this their own insights and concerns. Like other poststructuralist writers, they approach their work with an eye toward understanding and critiquing dynamics of power and knowledge; government direction and control of pedagogical and research processes; and constraints on human freedom, creativity, and diversity (difference). These issues are as salient for educational research today as they have ever been.

REFERENCES

Barthes, Roland. 1977. "Writers, Intellectuals, Teachers." Pp. 378–403 in *Roland Barthes: Selected Writings*. Edited by Susan Sontag. New York: Fontana.

Derrida, Jacques. 1983. "The Principles of Reason: The University in the Eyes of Its Pupils." *Diacritics* 13, 3 (Fall): 3–20.

Leitch, Vincent. 1996. *Postmodernism—Local Effects, Global Flows*. New York: State University of New York Press.

Lyotard, Jean-François. 1984. *The Postmodern Condition: A Report on Knowledge*. Translated by Geoff Bennington and Brian Massumi with a foreword by Fredric Jameson. Minneapolis: University of Minnesota Press.

Ulmer, Gregory. 1985. *Applied Grammatology: Post(e)-Pedagogy from Jacques Derrida to Joseph Beuys*. Baltimore, Md., and London: Johns Hopkins University Press.

1

What Is Poststructuralism?

In this introductory chapter we provide an account of poststructuralism, distinguishing it from postmodernism and from its predecessor movement, structuralism. It is important to devote some space to defining "postmodernism" because the term is often confused or deliberately conflated with "poststructuralism." While the two movements overlap philosophically and historically, it is important to distinguish between them in order to appreciate their respective intellectual genealogies and their theoretical relevance today. For the purposes of this chapter we argue that an important set of theoretical and historical differences can be most easily understood by recognizing the difference between their *theoretical objects of study*. Each movement is an attempt to supersede in various ways something that came before. Poststructuralism takes as its theoretical object "structuralism," whereas postmodernism takes as its theoretical object "modernism." Poststructuralism, in particular, ought to be seen as a specific philosophical response—strongly motivated by the work of Friedrich Nietzsche and Martin Heidegger—against the social scientific pretensions of structuralism. Postmodernism is sometimes used to describe similar views, but really has a much broader scope of application.

Our main argument for the latter part of this chapter is that the theoretical development of French structuralism during the late 1950s and 1960s led to the institutionalization of a transdisciplinary "mega-paradigm" based around the centrality of language and its scientific analysis in human social and cultural life, considered as self-reflexive signifying or semiotic systems or subsystems. It was, in this sense, part of the broader "linguistic turn" taken by Western philosophy. The tradition of structuralist linguistics has its origins in late-nineteenth-century European formalism; under the combined influence of Ferdinand de Saussure and Roman Jakobson, it developed into the dominant research program in linguistics. Unlike modernism, structuralism was never predominantly based upon an artistic performance, practice, or aesthetics. Rather, it began and developed as a form of literary criticism and linguistic analysis of discourse that permitted the scientific analysis of language as a differential system with no positive terms—*a science of structures* that undermined traditional humanist and romantic assumptions about intentionality, creativity, and "the speaker's/author's meaning." Then, in the hands of Claude Lévi-Strauss, A. J. Greimas, Roland Barthes, Louis Althusser, Jacques Lacan, Michel Foucault, and many others, structuralism made its way into anthropology, literary criticism, psychoanalysis, Marxism, history, aesthetic theory, and studies of popular culture, developing into a powerful overarching framework for the semiotic and linguistic analysis of society, economy, and culture, considered as a series of functionally interrelated sign systems.

We shall interpret poststructuralism, therefore, as a specifically *philosophical* response to the alleged scientific status of structuralism—to its status as a mega-paradigm for the social sciences—and as a movement that, under the inspiration of Nietzsche, Heidegger, and others, sought to decenter the "structures," the systematicity and scientific status of structuralism, to critique its underlying metaphysics and to extend it in a number of different directions, while at the same time preserving central elements of structuralism's critique of the humanist subject. In this argument and analysis we draw upon the work of Alan Schrift, who argues that one of the most important *differences* between the discourses of structuralism and poststructuralism is the renewal of philosophical discourse: "The structuralist rediscovery of Freud and Marx, along with Heidegger's retrieval of Nietzsche, set the stage for the emergence of poststructuralism as a distinctly *philosophical* response to the privileging of the human sciences that characterized the work of the structuralists" (1995: 4).

The influence of the first-generation poststructuralists has been immense: Inside France it has led to exciting developments at the forefront of feminist research, psychoanalysis, literary theory, anthropology, sociology, and history. It has also led to important crossfertilizations among the disciplines and to intellectual advances in newly configured fields such as film theory, media studies, queer theory, postcolonial studies, and Afro-American and Hellenistic studies. Outside France and especially in the American academy, the influence of poststructuralism has been strong in literary studies (for example, Jonathan Culler, Shoshana Felman, Vincent Leitch) and in the work of the Yale literary school (Paul de Man, Hillis Miller). Within the Western academy more generally it has influenced the traditional disciplines of sociology (Zygmunt Bauman, Barry Smart), philosophy (Cornel West, Paul Patton, Hubert

Dreyfus), politics (Colin Gordon, William Connolly, Barry Hindess), anthropology (James Clifford, Paul Rabinow), history (Hayden White, Mark Poster, Dominick La Capra), and geography (Edward Soja, David Harvey), as well as the newly emergent fields of feminist and gender studies (Judith Butler, Chris Weedon), postcolonial studies (Edward Said, Gayatri Spivak, Homi Bhabha), and cultural studies (Stuart Hall, Simon During).

But first, in this opening section of the chapter, we want to clarify what we mean by modernism and postmodernism, and distinguish that binary from the relation of structuralism to poststructuralism.

MODERNISM AND POSTMODERNISM

We begin with the term "modernism," which has two uses: The first refers to movements in the arts from around the end of the nineteenth century; the second is more historical and philosophical, referring to "the modern"—meaning "modernity"—the age or period following the medieval period. There is a relationship between these two senses that can be expressed simply by saying that "the modern" and "modernism" involve a *self-conscious break* with the old, the classical, and the traditional, and an emphasis on the new or the present. It also involves the general belief, contrary to classicism or traditionalism, that the modern is in some sense better than the old. Philosophically speaking, modernism in philosophy begins with the Renaissance—with the thought of Francis Bacon in England and René Descartes in France.

"Modernism," in the first sense of referring to developments in the arts from the end of the nineteenth century, typically is used to characterize the method, style, or attitude of modern artists, and, in particular, a style in which the artist deliberately breaks away from classical and traditional methods of expression based on assumptions of realism and naturalism. One author describes modernism in the following terms:

> Modernism in art, literature, and philosophy involved novelty, break with tradition, progress, continuous development, knowledge derived from either the position of the subject or from claims to objectivity. . . . [It] involved a shift . . . to the stream of consciousness, lived and internal time-consciousness, transcendental subjectivity, narrated remembrance and awareness. (Silverman, 1996: 353)

In philosophy (and theology), modernism can be seen as a movement sustained by a belief in the advancement of knowledge and human progress, made on the basis of experience and scientific method. It is epitomized, perhaps, by Immanuel Kant's "critical" philosophy and by the idea that advancement in knowledge comes with subjecting traditional beliefs to criticism. The American literary critic Clement Greenberg defined modernism as the historical tendency of an art practice toward complete self-referential autonomy. He writes in his famous essay "Modernist Painting":

> I identify Modernism with the intensification, almost the exacerbation, of this self-critical tendency that began with the philosopher Kant. Because he was the first to criticize the means itself of criticism, I conceive of Kant as the first real Modernist. The essence of Modernism lies, as I see it, in the use of the characteristic methods of a discipline to criticize itself—not in order to subvert it, but to entrench it more firmly in its area of competence. Kant used logic to establish the limits of logic, and while he withdrew much from its old jurisdiction, logic was left in all the more secure possession of what remained to it. (1973: 66)

M. H. Abrams (1981) suggests that modernism involves a self-conscious and radical break with the traditional bases of Western culture and Western art and that the precursors of this break are artists and thinkers who questioned our cultural certainties, including Western conceptions of the self.

Postmodernism, thus, has two general meanings related to these different senses of the term modernism: It can be used, aesthetically, to refer specifically to developments in the arts subsequent to or in reaction to modernism; or, in a historical and philosophical sense, to refer to a period—"postmodernity"—or its ethos. Postmodernism, in the first sense, grows out of the context of aesthetic high modernism, the history of the Western avant-garde, and, in particular, the artistic innovation and experimentalism that followed the crisis of representation that took place with cubism, Dadaism, and surrealism, the process of increasing abstraction thereafter (suprematism, constructivism, abstract expressionism, minimalism), and, finally, the abandoning of the aesthetic process completely, with Marcel Duchamp's "readymades," Josef Beuys's installations, Andy Warhol's silkscreen mechanical reproductions, and the movement known as conceptualism.

In the second sense, it could be argued that postmodernism represents a transformation of modernity or a radical shift in the system of values and practices underlying modernity. For example, one scholar, speaking of its application to the human sciences generally, suggests:

> Postmodernism can be recognized by two key assumptions. First, the assumption that there is no common denominator—in "nature" or "truth" or "God" or "the future"—that guarantees either the One-ness of the world or the possibility of natural or objective thought. Second, the assumption that all human systems operate like language, being self-reflexive rather than referential systems—systems of differential function which are powerful but finite, and which construct and maintain meaning and value. (Ermarth, 1996: 587)

Another scholar discusses postmodernism's relevance to political philosophy:

> Postmodernism aims at exposing how, in modern, liberal democracies, the construction of political identity and the operationalization of basic values take place through the deployment of conceptual binaries such as we/them, responsible/irresponsible, rational/irrational, legitimate/illegitimate, normal/abnormal, and so on. . . . [P]ostmodernists draw attention to the ways in which the boundary between . . . [these] terms is socially reproduced and policed. (Lilly, 1998: 591)

Matters become more complex when "poststructuralist" thinkers began to systematically engage the term "postmodernism." An influential definition of postmodernism, and one of the most debated, comes from the poststructuralist thinker Jean-François Lyotard, who in his celebrated *The Postmodern Condition: A Report on Knowledge* ([1979] 1984) analyzed the status of knowledge in the most advanced societies in ways that many critics believed signaled a break not only with the so-called modern era but also with various traditionally "modern" ways of viewing the world. He writes in a now famous formulation: "I will use the term *modern* to designate any science that legitimates itself with reference to a metadiscourse . . . making explicit appeal to some grand narrative, such as the dialectics of the Spirit, the hermeneutics of meaning, the emancipation of the rational or working subject, or the creation of wealth" (Lyotard, 1984: xxii).

By contrast, Lyotard defines "postmodern" simply as "incredulity toward metanarratives" (1984: xxiv). In *The Postmodern Condition*, he was concerned with the grand narratives that had grown out of the Enlightenment and had come to mark modernity. In *The Postmodern Explained to Children*, Lyotard mentions specifically: "the progressive emancipation of reason and freedom, the progressive or catastrophic emancipation of labour . . . , the enrichment of all through the progress of capitalist technoscience, and even . . . the salvation of creatures through the conversion of souls to the Christian narrative of martyred love" (1992: 29). Grand narratives, then, are the stories that cultures tell themselves about their own practices and beliefs in order to legitimate them. They function as a unified single story that purports to justify a set of practices, a cultural self-image, a discourse or an institution (see Peters, 1995).

Lyotard, in his very first footnote of *The Postmodern Condition*, acknowledged the sources for his notion of "the postmodern": the sociology of postindustrial society (he mentions the work of Daniel Bell and Alain Touraine), the literary criticism of Ihab Hassan, and studies of "performance" in postmodern culture by Michel Benamou, Charles Caramello, and M. Köhler. These are useful sources to note because, taken together, they combine elements of the changing mode of economic and social organization of advanced societies with certain changes in culture. Lyotard's innovation as a theorist was to bring together under a narrative analysis elements that were previously kept discrete—that is, the economic (postindustrial) and the cultural (postmodern). He suggested that the status of knowledge is altered as societies enter the postindustrial age and cultures enter the postmodern age, actively indicating a structural homology between changes to the economic and cultural modes without assigning priority to one over the other (as Marxists do). Some sociologists have begun to talk of this transition in terms of "postmodernization," just as sociologists of a previous generation analyzed the transition from the traditional to the modern in terms of "modernization." Postmodernization implies a critique of development theory as a single and sequenced set of stages based upon a standard yardstick of Western industrialization. It offers the possibilities of stages of development that are neither invariant nor necessary and may include non-Western preferred ways of taking advantage of new information and communications technologies as a basis for the knowledge of economy and society.

Still, Lyotard is often misunderstood as saying that postmodernism somehow "surpasses" or supersedes modernism. On the contrary, he says that postmodernism is "not modernism at its end but in the nascent state, and this state is constant. I have said and will say again the postmodern signifies not the end of modernism, but another relation to modernism" (1984: 79). What Lyotard suggests is that postmodernism is *a continuation of modernism by other means*—the search for the new, the avant-garde, and the experimental remain. In other words, considered a category in aesthetics, postmodernism entertains an ambivalent relation to modernism; it defines a style, an attitude, or an ethos rather than a period (that is, something that comes *after* modernism). In this sense, there are clearly many postmodernisms—definitions of artistic styles that may come and go. *Descriptive not temporal*

STRUCTURALISM AND POSTSTRUCTURALISM

A Decade of French Structuralism, 1958–1968

French structuralism had its origins in the development of structural linguistics that took place at the hands of Ferdinand de Saussure and Roman Jakobson at the turn of the century. Saussure offered a course in general linguistics between 1907 and 1911; after his death in 1913 students published his work reconstructed from their notes as *Cours de linguistique* in 1916. Translated as *Course in General Linguistics* (1974), this book established the systematic nature of signification in language and the relational definition of its elements. Saussure distinguished his "scientific" or synchronic approach against the prevailing historical, developmental, or diachronic study of languages through his distinction between *la parole*—actual speech or speech events—and *la langue*—the formal language system that governs speech events. Saussure was interested in the function of linguistic elements rather than their cause. For instance, he defined words as a "sign" comprising a concept and a sound—the signified and the signifier—that do not *cause* one another, but are functionally related, each depending upon the other. For example, hearing the word/sound "dog" does not *cause* the listener to think of a concept or idea of a dog. The relationship of signifier to signified is entirely arbitrary, defined only as a function of differences within the system. There is nothing in the world that causes a sound to be associated with a particular concept, as the fact that different languages have different signifiers for the same signified (or concept) testifies. Jonathan Culler explains this *structuralist* view of language:

> [It is] not simply that a language is a system of elements which are wholly defined by their relations to one another within the system, though it is that, but that the linguistic system consists of different levels of structure; at each level one can identify elements which contrast with one another and combine with other elements to form higher-level units, and the principles of structure at each level are fundamentally the same. (1976: 49)

In this system, *difference* plays a crucial role, and, as we will see, this idea plays a central part in the later development of poststructuralist thought. Saussure argued: "*In language there are only differences*. Even more important: a difference generally implies positive terms between which the difference is set up; but in language, there are differences *without positive terms*" (1974: 120). It is the *difference* between signifiers that permits them to function as such. In this model Saussure sought to establish a *general* science of signs—*semiology*, the "study of the life of signs within society"—that became central to all the human sciences (see Gadet, 1989). In other words, the signifier/signified relation can be found not only in formal language per se, but also in other aspects of society and culture (such as styles of dress, body language, architecture, and so on). This broader link was secured through the work of Roman Jakobson, making Saussure's views more widely known and giving birth to twentieth-century structuralism (see Selden, 1995).

Jakobson was a central influence on the historical development of structural linguistics. He was an instrumental figure in Russian Formalism, helping to set up both the Moscow Linguistic Circle and the Society for the Study of Poetic Language (OPOJAZ) in St. Petersburg before moving to Czechoslovakia in 1920 to establish the Prague Linguistic Circle. Linda R. Waugh and Monique Monville-Burston suggest that "The strongest influence on

Jakobson's thinking was the turbulent artistic movement of the early twentieth century . . . , including the work of the literary and artistic avant-garde: Picasso, Braque, Stravinsky, Joyce, Xlebnikov, Le Corbusier" (1990: 4).

In fact, it was Jakobson who first coined the term "structuralism" in 1929 to designate a structural-functional approach to the scientific investigation of phenomena, the basic task of which was to reveal the inner laws of the system:

> Were we to comprise the leading idea of present-day science in its most various manifestations, we could hardly find a more appropriate designation than *structuralism*. Any set of phenomena examined by contemporary science is treated not as a mechanical agglomeration but as a structural whole, and the basic task is to reveal the inner, whether static or developmental, laws of this system. What appears to be the focus of scientific preoccupations is no longer the outer stimulus, but the internal premises of the development: now the mechanical conception of processes yields to the question of their functions. (Jakobson, 1973: 11)

It is important to note that Jakobson defined his theory of language structure *against* Saussure's, which he found both too abstract and static. Influenced strongly by Hegel, Jakobson treated Saussure's dichotomous formulations (*langue/parole*, synchrony/diachrony) dialectically, insisting on the close relationship between form and meaning within a state of dynamic synchrony (Waugh and Monville-Burston, 1990: 9).

In what proved to be an historic moment of influence, Jakobson introduced Claude Lévi-Strauss to structural linguistics at the New School for Social Research in New York in the early 1940s. Lévi-Strauss then published an article relating structural linguistics and ethnology for the first time in Jakobson's newly established journal *Word* in 1945. That article became an early chapter of *Anthropologie Structurale*, published in 1958 (and published in English as *Structural Anthropology* in 1968). Lévi-Strauss acknowledged his debt to Saussure and Jakobson and proceeded to describe a method in anthropology focusing upon the notion of *unconscious structure*:

> If, as we believe to be the case, the unconscious activity of the mind consists in imposing forms upon content, and if these forms are fundamentally the same for all minds—ancient and modern, primitive and civilized . . . —it is necessary and sufficient to grasp the unconscious structure underlying each institution and custom, in order to obtain a principle of interpretation valid for other institutions and other customs. (1968: 21)

Lévi-Strauss suggested that we apprehend this unconscious structure through the employment of the method developed by structural linguistics, declaring that "Structural linguistics will certainly play the same renovating role with respect to the social sciences that nuclear physics, for example, has played for the physical sciences" (1968: 33). Lévi-Strauss went on to define the structural method in terms of the programmatic statement made by Nikolai Troubetzkoy (a member of Jakobson's Prague Linguistic School) in his seminal *Principles of Phonology*:

> First, structural linguistics shifts from the study of *conscious* linguistic phenomena to the study of their *unconscious* infrastructure; second, it does not treat *terms* as independent entities, taking instead as its basis of analysis the *relations* between terms; third, it introduces the concept of *system* . . . ; finally, structural linguistics aims at discovering *general laws*, either by induction [or deduction]. (1968: 33)

In other words, in the same way that language is structured by a grammar and other rules that allow us to organize our speech intelligibly, *even when we are not aware of and cannot articulate those structures*, so too are cultures and societies organized by structures that the participants may not be aware of, but which nevertheless give their social practices and institutions coherence and meaning. Employing this viewpoint, Lévi-Strauss suggested that social science would be able to formulate necessary relationships ("new perspectives . . . open up") where, for example, the anthropologist can study kinship systems in the same way that a linguist studies phonemes: "Like phonemes, kinship terms are elements of meaning; like phonemes, they acquire meaning only if they are integrated into systems," and kinship systems, like phonemic systems, "are built by the mind on the level of unconscious thought" (1968: 34). Three years later in 1961, in his inaugural lecture at the Collège de France, Lévi-Strauss publicly recognized his debt to Saussure and defined anthropology as a branch of semiology.

After the publication of *Anthropologie Structurale* the structuralist revolution flourished in France, especially during the 1960s: Roland Barthes, introduced to linguistics by A. J. Greimas in the early fifties, published his *Mythologies* in 1957 and became Directeur d'études in the "sociology of signs, symbols and representations" at the École des Hautes Études in 1962; Philippe Sollers founded the avant-garde literary journal *Tel Quel* in 1960; and Michel Foucault published *Folie et deraison: histoire de la folie a l'age classique* in 1961. In 1963 Louis Althusser invited Jacques Lacan to hold his seminar at the École Normale and the productive dialogue between Marxism and psychoanalysis began; the year 1966 saw the publication of Louis Althusser's *Pour Marx*, Foucault's *Les mots et les choses*, and Lacan's *Écrits* (see Dosse, 1997). The structuralist revolution in France, across a range of disciplines, reached its peak.

Psychologist Jean Piaget published his book *Structuralism* ([1968] 1971) when the structuralist bubble in France had already burst because structuralism was identified with outdated and suspect political attitudes. Many interpreted the spontaneous events of May 1968 as a refutation of the structuralist critique of bourgeois humanism. Piaget's *Structuralism* is, nevertheless, both interesting and useful in defining structuralism:

> As a first approximation, we may say that a structure is a system of transformations. Inasmuch as it is a system and not a mere collection of elements and their properties, these transformations involve laws: the structure is preserved or enriched by the interplay of its transformation laws, which never yield results external to the system nor employ elements that are external to it. In short, the notion of structure is comprised of three key ideas: the idea of wholeness, the idea of transformation, and the idea of self-regulation. (1971: 5)

The notion of wholeness emerges from the distinction between *structures* and *aggregates*. Only the former are wholes, whereas the latter are formed of elements that are independent of the complexes into which they enter: "The elements of a structure are subordinated to laws, and it is in terms of these laws that the structure *qua* whole or system is defined" (1971: 7). The nature of structured wholes depends upon their laws of composition that in turn govern the transformations of the system, whether they be mathematical (e.g., 1+1 "makes" 2) or temporal. This notion of self-regulation entails both self-maintenance and closure and Piaget mentions three basic mechanisms of self-regulation: rhythm (as in biology), regulation (in the cybernetic sense), and operation (in the sense of logic).

Piaget, then, emphasized the scientific study of structures and their capacity to give a complete and lawlike explanation of phenomena under consideration. Piaget discussed in turn: mathematical structures, physical and biological structures, psychological structures (Gestalt psychology, the genesis of intelligence), linguistic structuralism (including Chomsky's generative grammar), structural analysis in the social sciences (focusing on Lévi-Strauss's structural anthropology), and structuralism and philosophy.

In the chapter "Structuralism and Philosophy" Piaget questioned less scientific and systematic versions of structuralism, calling Foucault's *Les mots et les choses* "structuralism without structures" because "there cannot be a coherent structuralism apart from constructivism" (1971: 135). He complained that rather than positing structures Foucault talks of *epistemes* tied to language, and argued that for Foucault the human sciences are nothing more than the outcomes of mutations of *epistemes* that follow one another in time but according to no preordained or necessary sequence. Such an archaeology of the human sciences spells the end of man, because it de-emphasizes human agency and subjectivity. In his conclusion Piaget specifically addressed this most radical part of Foucault's work:

"Structures" have not been the death of the *subject* or its activities. . . . In the first place, structuralism calls for a differentiation between *individual subject* . . . , and *epistemic subject*. . . . In the second place, the always fragmentary and frequently distorting grasp of consciousness must be set apart from the achievements of the subject; what he knows is the *outcome* of his intellectual activity, not its mechanisms. (1971: 139)

What is interesting about this characterization, which from Piaget's standpoint made Foucault a bad structuralist, is that from Foucault's standpoint he wasn't trying to be a structuralist at all. Reflecting back on these debates, Foucault, in a rare interview, directly engaged the question of structuralism and poststructuralism, making it clear that structuralism was *not* a French invention and that the French version of structuralism during the 1960s should be properly viewed against the background of European formalism. Foucault suggested that apart from those who applied structural methods in linguistics and comparative mythology none of the protagonists in the structuralist movement knew very clearly what they were doing. In fact, Foucault famously declared, he *never was* a structuralist, although he acknowledged that the problem addressed by structuralism was a problem very close to his interests as he defined them on a number of occasions: "that of the subject and the recasting of the subject" (1983: 205). In this sense, Foucault might be seen as a key transitional figure between structuralism and poststructuralism (although he denied being a poststructuralist as well!).

THE EMERGENCE OF POSTSTRUCTURALISM

Poststructuralism can be characterized as a mode of thinking, a style of philosophizing, and a kind of writing, yet the term should not be used to convey a sense of homogeneity, singularity, or unity. The very term "poststructuralism" is contested. Mark Poster, for example, (1989: 6) remarks that the term "poststructuralism" is American in origin and that "poststructuralist theory" names a uniquely American practice, based upon an assimilation of the work of a diverse range of theorists. More generally, we might agree that the term is a label primarily used by the English-speaking academic community to describe a distinctively philosophical response to the type of structuralism characterizing the work of Claude Lévi-Strauss (anthropology), Louis Althusser (Marxism), Jacques Lacan (psychoanalysis), and Roland Barthes (literature). Manfred Frank (1988), a contemporary German philosopher, for his part prefers the term "neostructuralism," emphasizing more of a continuity with "structuralism," as does John Sturrock, who, focusing on Jacques Derrida (*the* "post-Structuralist"— indeed, "the weightiest and most acute critic Structuralism has had"), discusses the "post" in "post-Structuralism" in terms of "coming after and of seeking to extend Structuralism in its rightful direction" (1986: 137). He continues, "post-Structuralism is a critique of Structuralism conducted from within: that is, it turns certain of Structuralism's arguments against itself and points to certain fundamental inconsistencies in their method which Structuralists have ignored." Richard Harland (1987), by contrast, coins the term "super-structuralism" as a single umbrella based on an underlying framework of assumptions common to "Structuralists, Poststructuralists, (European) Semioticians, Althusserian Marxists, Lacanians, Foucauldians, *et al*" (Harland, 1993: ix–x).

All of these locutions regard as central the movement's historical, institutional, and theoretical proximity to "structuralism." Yet poststructuralism cannot be simply reduced to a set of shared assumptions, a method, a theory, or even a school. It is best referred to as a *movement of thought*—a complex skein of thought embodying different forms of critical practice. It is decidedly interdisciplinary and has many different but related strands.

As a French and predominantly Parisian affair, first-generation poststructuralism is inseparable from the immediate intellectual milieu that prevailed in postwar France, a history dominated by diverse intellectual forces: the legacy of Alexander Kojéve and Jean Hyppolite's "existentialist" interpretations of Hegel's *Phenomenology*; Heidegger's phenomenology of Being and Jean-Paul Sartre's existentialism; Jacques Lacan's rediscovery and structuralist "reading" of Freud; the omnipresence of Georges Bataille and Maurice Blanchot; Gaston Bachelard's radical epistemology and Georges Canguilhem's studies of science; and, perhaps most important, the French reception of Friedrich Nietzsche.

Decisive for the emergence of poststructuralism was, undoubtedly, the rediscovery of Nietzsche's writings (and Martin Heidegger's interpretation of them) by a group of French thinkers, along with their structuralist readings of both Freud and Marx. Where Marx was seen to play out the theme of power in his work, and Freud gave a conceptual priority to the notion of desire, Nietzsche was read as a philosopher who did not prioritize or subordinate one concept over the other. His philosophy offered a way forward that combined an examination of both power and desire.

Nietzsche's philosophy offered a critique of truth and an emphasis upon the plurality of interpretation; it stressed the idea of *style* and the way in which style is central both philosophically and aesthetically in overcoming oneself in a process of perpetual self-becoming; and it emphasized relations of power and knowledge through the concept of the "will to power" and its manifestations as will to truth and will to knowledge. The French poststructuralists adopted these themes and experimented with them in novel ways. Foucault, for instance, developed Nietzschean genealogy as a form of critical history that resists the search for origins and essences but focuses instead upon notions of *descent* and *emergence*. Lyotard developed Nietzsche's aversion to the universalizing tendencies of modern philosophy by analyzing the pragmatics of language through the use of narratives and narratology. Derrida, following Nietzsche, Heidegger, and Saussure, challenges the assumptions that govern binary or oppositional thinking, demonstrating how binary oppositions always support a hierarchy or economy of value that operates by subordinating one term to another, and, through deconstruction, revealing, unraveling, and reversing such hierarchies.

All these thinkers together emphasize the way meaning is an active construction radically dependent upon the pragmatics of context and, thereby, challenge the universality of truth claims. Foucault, for example, regards truth as a product of discursive regimes or genres, each with its own irreducible body of rules for constituting well-formed sentences or statements. Following Nietzsche, they all question the Cartesian-Kantian *humanistic* subject as an autonomous, free, and transparently self-conscious subject that is the fount of all knowledge and moral and political agency. By contrast, and following Nietzsche's critique of liberal philosophy, they increasingly come to specify the subject in all its historical and cultural complexity as "decentered" within the language system, as discursively constituted, and as positioned at the intersection of libidinal forces and sociocultural practices. The subject is seen as *embodied* and *engendered*, physiologically speaking, as a *temporal* being who comes into existence and faces death and extinction as a body, yet is also as malleable, infinitely flexible, and subject to the practices and strategies of normalization and individualization that characterize modern institutions (such as schools—this point, of course, has been a prime area of inquiry for poststructuralist scholars in education).

Moreover, Gilles Deleuze's ([1962] 1983) *Nietzsche and Philosophy*, a pivotal text that interpreted Nietzsche's philosophy as an attack upon the Hegelian dialectic, helped to create the conditions for a theoretical stress upon pure difference—a "philosophy of difference"—that emphasized difference not only as a constant in linguistic and symbolic systems but also as a necessary element in the process of creating social and cultural identity (see Peters, 1996, 1998). We return to this theme at length, below.

In its first (French) generation, poststructuralism was exemplified in the work and writings of Jacques Derrida, Michel Foucault, Julia Kristeva, Jean-François Lyotard, Gilles Deleuze, Luce Irigaray, Jean Baudrillard and many others. Historically, its early formation and institutional development can be charted in Philippe Soller's highly influential journal *Tel Quel*, and there are strong connections with literary figures such as Maurice Blanchot and Roland

Barthes. Poststructuralist thinkers have developed distinctive forms of analysis (grammatology, deconstruction, archaeology, genealogy, semanalysis) and often worked these forms into critiques of specific institutions (such as the family, state, prison, clinic, school, factory, armed forces, university, even philosophy itself) and as theoretical frameworks for understanding a range of different media (reading, writing, teaching, television, the visual arts, the plastic arts, film, and forms of electronic communication).

The American reception of deconstruction and the influential formulation of "poststructuralism" in the English-speaking world quickly became institutionalized from the point at which Derrida delivered his essay "Structure, Sign, and Play in the Discourse of the Human Sciences" to the International Colloquium on Critical Languages and the Sciences of Man at John Hopkins University in October 1966. Richard Macksey and Eugenio Donato described the conference as "the first time in the United States that structuralist thought had been considered as a crossdisciplinary phenomenon" (1970: x). Even before the conclusion of the conference, there were clear signs that the ruling transdisciplinary paradigm of structuralism had been superseded, yet only a paragraph in Macksey's "Concluding Remarks" signaled the importance of Derrida's "radical reappraisals of our [structuralist] assumptions" (1970: 320). In this now-classic essay, "Structure, Sign, and Play," Derrida questioned the "structurality of structure" or the notion of a "center" that, he argued, served to limit the play of structure:

> The entire history of the concept of structure . . . must be thought of as a series of substitutions of center for center, as a linked chain of determinations of the center. Successively, and in a regulated fashion, the center receives different forms or names. The history of metaphysics, like the history of the West, is the history of these metaphors and metonymies. Its matrix . . . is the determination of being as *presence* in all senses of this word. It could be shown that all the names related to fundamentals, to principles, or to the center have always designated an invariable presence—*eidos, arche, telos, energeia, ousia* (essence, existence, substance, subject) *aletheia*, transcendentality, consciousness, God, man, and so forth. (1978: 279–80)

In this one paragraph Derrida called into question both the previous decade of French structuralism and intimated the directions of his own intellectual ambitions.

The "decentering" of structure, of the transcendental signified, and of the *sovereign* subject, Derrida suggests—naming his three sources of inspiration—can be found in (1) the Nietzschean critique of metaphysics and, especially, of the concepts of being and truth, (2) in the Freudian critique of self-presence, as Derrida says, "the critique of consciousness, of the subject, of self-identity and of self-proximity or self-possession" (1978: 280), and, (3) more radically, in the Heideggerian destruction of metaphysics, "of the determination of Being as presence" (1978: 280). In the rest of the essay, Derrida considers the theme of "decentering" in relation to Lévi-Strauss' ethnology and concludes by distinguishing two interpretations of structure. One, Hegelian in origin and exemplified in Lévi-Strauss's work, he argues, "dreams of deciphering a truth or an origin which escapes play and the order of the sign" and seeks the "inspiration of a new humanism." The other, "which is no longer turned toward the origin, affirms play and tries to pass beyond man and humanism" (1978: 292). Humanism as a central motif of European liberal thought tended to anchor all analysis and theory in the "centered" subject while structuralism came to regard subjects as simply bearers of structures. The poststructuralists in various ways do continue to advance the structuralist understanding of the subject in relational terms as an element within structures and systems; yet they also question the philosophical construction of the subject in terms of specific histories—the questioning of the Cartesian-Kantian subject, the questioning of the Hegelian and phenomenological subject, the questioning of the subject of existentialism, the questioning of the Marxian collective subject.

STRUCTURALISM AND POSTSTRUCTURALISM: AFFINITIES

Clearly, poststructuralism shares some concerns in common with structuralism, but it also differs from it in certain respects. In this and the next sections we discuss both poststructuralism's affinities and continuities with structuralism and its theoretical innovations and differences.

Affinities with Structuralism

We shall begin with the critique of Renaissance humanist philosophy and its conception of the rational, autonomous, self-transparent, human subject. Poststructuralism shares with structuralism a suspicion of the privileging of human consciousness by phenomenology and existentialism. Both entertain a skepticism about human consciousness as autonomous, as directly accessible, and as the primary basis of historical understanding and action. Phenomenology and existentialism inherited the legacy of Renaissance humanist thought, which assumed that there is a stable, coherent, knowable self who knows both itself and the world through reason. This humanist tradition, at least in the modern era, dating from Bacon and Descartes, emphasized a "scientific" mode of knowledge, produced by an objective, rational self, that can provide universal truths about the world. Such scientific knowledge can be applied to all human institutions and practices and is considered the ultimate basis of what is true, and therefore of what is right and good. Like the humanist tradition, phenomenology and existentialism assumed a rational, individual, autonomous, and self-present subject. Structuralism represents a reaction to such subjectivism and its ideals of personal freedom and historical agency. Poststructuralism, like structuralism, entertained a suspicion of self-knowledge (as expressed by Hegel, for example), suggesting that sociocultural structures played an important role in forming self-consciousness.

Heidegger's investigation into "subjectivity" was also crucial for poststructuralism. He argued that "being-in-the-world" (the distinctively human mode of existence) precedes the subject's self-knowledge and autonomy. In his famous "Letter on Humanism," Heidegger explicitly denied that his hermeneutical phenomenology is a kind of humanism. Like the poststructuralists, Heidegger questioned philosophies of the subject that do not take into account the external conditions of the subject's possibilities. More recently, humanism's emphasis on absolute self-consciousness and its alleged universalism have come to be regarded as socially exclusive and, ultimately, oppressive of the other—of social and cultural groups and individuals who operate with different cultural criteria. Poststructuralism emphasizes the discursive constitution of self (and self-regulation)—its corporeality, its temporality and finitude, its unconscious and libidinal energies, and the historical and cultural location of the subject. For example, Foucault in his early work explored the historical conditions that make possible certain kinds of subjectivity and agency and also the production of *modern* individualized subjects in institutions such as the prison, the hospital, and the school.

We can also identify between structuralism and poststructuralism a shared theoretical understanding of language and culture in terms of linguistic and symbolic *systems*, where the interrelations of constituent elements are regarded as more important than the elements considered in isolation from one another. Both structuralism and poststructuralism take up the Saussurean belief that linguistic signs act reflexively rather than referentially. Systems of value work through the self-reflexive operation of *differences*, and most symbolic or coded systems of meaning (e.g., city, fashion, school, classroom), can be analyzed in similar semiotic terms. Poststructuralist thought has developed a range of different methods or approaches (e.g., archaeology, genealogy, deconstruction) that operate according to their own logics but tend to emphasize notions of difference, local determinacy, historical breaks or discontinuities, serialization, repetition, and a mode of critique as "dismantling" or "disassembling" (read, deconstruction). Sometimes this is taken to indicate anti-realism about meaning and reference, involving a rejection of the picture of knowledge as an accurate representation and truth as correspondence to reality.

Poststructuralists do display—especially in relation to literature—a greater textual self-awareness and a complex understanding of the importance of *style* to both philosophy and the human sciences. These thinkers, acknowledging their debt to Jakobson, have developed highly innovative and sophisticated philosophical strategies and approaches for the analysis of texts, text analogues, histories, and cultures. In particular, the contemporary importance of narrative theory and "narratology" owe their popularity to structuralist and poststructuralist modes of analysis.

Structuralism and poststructuralism also generally share a belief in the unconscious and in hidden structures or sociohistorical forces that, to a large extent, constrain and govern our behavior. Much of this shared understanding can be directly indebted to the influence of Freud. Freud's study of the unconscious and his clinical investigations undermined the prevalent philosophical view of the pure rationality and self-transparency of the subject, substituting a greater complexity that called into question traditional distinctions of reason and unreason (or madness)—recall Foucault's first book. Much of the present emphasis within poststructuralist thought on the subject of desire, the body, and sexuality is also due to Freud's influence. Jacques Lacan, returning to the critical spirit of Freud, offers a structuralist reading emphasizing the logico-linguistic structural conditions underlying the individual as a subject of desire and language. Rather than regarding the subject as self-possessed (as in the Anglo-American tradition of psychoanalysis), Lacan regards the self in relation to language. His famous formulation "The unconscious is structured as a language" indicates that the unconscious has a structure that can be decoded and read like a language. This represents Lacan's return to Freud by way of Saussure. As one author writes, "Lacan's theory describes an inevitably *split* subject: a subject formed in the child's struggle to be represented by language as a speaker. The sexual specificity and desire of the resulting subject are irrevocable marks of this split or insufficiency" (Hengehold, 1998: 199). This inheritance, perhaps, goes some way to explaining the emphasis in the work of Foucault, Derrida, Lyotard, and Deleuze and Guattari, on subjects of desire and sexuality; and, more recently, a similar but more gender-critical emphasis in the work of French poststructural feminists, including Julia Kristeva and Luce Irigaray.

Hence we can distinguish a common intellectual inheritance and tradition based upon Saussure, Jakobson and the Russian formalists, Freud, and Marx, among other thinkers. This shared intellectual history is like a complex skein that has many strands. We might call it European Formalism, beginning in pre-revolutionary Russia, in Geneva, and in Jena, with simultaneous and overlapping developments in linguistics, poetics, art, science, and literature.

STRUCTURALISM AND POSTSTRUCTURALISM:
THEORETICAL INNOVATIONS AND DIFFERENCES

Where structuralism sought to efface history through more static, synchronic (point in time) analyses of structures, poststructuralism brings about a renewed interest in writing a critical history that emphasizes diachronic (changing over time) analyses; on mutation, transformation, and discontinuity of structures; on serialization, repetition, "archaeology"; and, perhaps most importantly, on what Foucault, using Nietzsche's term, calls "genealogy." Genealogical narratives are thought to replace ontology. Or, to express the same thought in a different way, questions of ontology (being) become historicized. Heidegger, if you recall, was making this fundamental point.

Poststructuralism challenges scientism in the human sciences, introducing an anti-foundationalism in epistemology and a new emphasis upon perspectivism in interpretation. The movement challenges the rationalism and realism that structuralism shares with positivism—with its Promethean faith in scientific method, in progress, and in the capacity of research to discern and identify *universal* structures of cultures and the human mind. One author writes:

> Post-structuralist critiques of structuralism are typically based on two fundamental theses: (1) that no system can be autonomous (self-sufficient) in the way that structuralism requires; and (2) that the defining dichotomies on which structuralist systems are based express distinctions that do not hold up under careful scrutiny. . . . Post-structuralists retain structuralism's elimination of the subject from any role as a foundation of reality or of our knowledge of it. But, in opposition to structuralism, they also reject any logical foundation for a system of thought (in, for example, its internal coherence). For post-structuralists, there is no foundation of any sort that can guarantee the validity or stability of any system of thought. (Gutting, 1998a: 597)

As Gutting goes on to explain, "the logical structure of a system requires that its concepts be unambiguously defined," which means that concepts are defined in terms of sharp dichotomies or binary oppositions (for example, the distinction in Saussure between signifier and signified). Poststructuralism challenges the status of such distinctions or dichotomies: They are neither foundational nor exclusive in the way that structuralists assume they are.

As commented previously, the rediscovery of Nietzsche, and Heidegger's interpretation of Nietzsche as the "last metaphysician," is highly significant for the emergence of poststructuralism. Nietzsche's work provided a new way to theorize and conceive of the discursive operation of power and desire in the constitution and self-overcoming of human subjects. Alan Schrift writes:

Nietzsche's critique of truth, his emphasis upon interpretation and differential relations of power, and his attention to questions of style in philosophical discourse became central motifs for the poststructuralists as they turned away from the human sciences and toward philosophical-critical analyses of: writing and textuality (Derrida); relations of power, discourse, and the construction of the subject (Foucault); desire and language (Deleuze); questions of aesthetic and political judgment (Jean-François Lyotard); and questions of sexual difference and gender construction (Luce Irigaray, Julia Kristeva, Hélène Cixous). (Schrift, 1996: 452)

Much of the history of poststructuralism can be written as a series of innovative theoretical developments of or about Heidegger's notion of technology. Heidegger's philosophy of technology is related to his critique of the history of Western metaphysics and the disclosure of being. The essence of technology is a poiesis, or "bringing forth," that is grounded in disclosure (*aletheia*). He suggested that the essence of modern technology shows itself in what he calls "enframing" and reveals itself as "standing reserve," a concept that refers to resources that are stored in the anticipation of consumption: for example, a river, once viewed as a potential source of electricity, through damming, can never be seen or understood simply as a river ever again—it has been "enframed" in a new way, as indeed humans themselves are also enframed in this new relation. At its extremes, all of Nature is viewed simply as a resource (a "standing reserve") for human consumption and use. As such, modern technology names the final stage in the history of metaphysics (nihilism) and the way in which *the* world is disclosed in this particular epoch: a stockpiling in principle completely knowable and devoted entirely for human use. Heidegger suggested that the essence of technology is nothing technological; it is rather a system (*Gestell*), an all-embracing view of technology, described as a mode of human existence that focuses upon the way machine technology can alter our mode of being, distorting our actions and aspirations. Heidegger was careful not to view this shift as either simply an optimist or pessimist; he saw his own work as preparation for a new beginning enabling one to escape from such nihilism and allowing the resolute individual to achieve authenticity.

This Heideggerian philosophy had a particularly strong influence upon both Derrida, in his ideas of destruction and deconstruction, absence and presence, and Foucault, whose various notions of technology in relation to the self spring conceptually from Heidegger. Heidegger's notion of technology is also central to the ways in which various poststructuralist thinkers have theorized the power of the new information and communications technologies ("cyberspace"), and media generally, to restructure and reconfigure our subjectivities and identities. Some of this critical work has been especially influential in the context of education (see Peters, 2002).

Poststructuralism, unlike structuralism, also has an interest in deepening democracy and in offering a political critique of Enlightenment values. It criticizes the ways that modern liberal democracies construct political identity on the basis of a series of binary oppositions (e.g., we/them, citizen/noncitizen, responsible/irresponsible, legitimate/illegitimate), which has the effect of excluding or "othering" some groups of people. For example, Western countries grant rights to citizens—rights that are dependent upon citizenship—and regard noncitizens, that is, immigrants, those seeking asylum, and refugees, as "aliens" without these rights. Some strands of poststructuralist thought are interested in examining how these boundaries are socially constructed and how they are maintained and policed. In particular, the deconstruction of political hierarchies of value, comprising binary oppositions and philosophies of difference, are seen as highly significant for current debates on multiculturalism and feminism. Philosophies of difference are also seen as impinging directly upon the universalist values of the (Eurocentric) political culture of the Enlightenment, questioning in particular the Enlightenment philosophical justifications of "rights" from the standpoint of the more genealogical and discursive construction of what count as "rights."

In addition, Foucault's later work, based on the notion of "governmentality," has initiated a substantial body of contemporary work in political philosophy dealing directly with political reason. Foucault coined this term, "governmentality," in an analysis of liberalism and neoliberalism, viewing the former as originating in a doctrine concerning the critique of state reason. Foucault used the term to mean the art of government (and of self-government) and to signal the emergence of a distinctive type of rule that became the basis of modern liberal politics. He maintained that the "art of government" emerged in the sixteenth century, motivated by diverse questions such as the government of oneself (personal conduct), the government of souls (pastoral doctrine), and the government of children (pedagogy). It is around the same time that the idea of "economy" was introduced into political practice as part of the governmentalization of the state. What is distinctive about Foucault's approach here, and in much of his work, is that he was interested in the question of *how* power comes to be exercised. Implicitly, he was providing a critique of contemporary tendencies to overvalue problems of the state, reducing it to a formal unity or singularity based upon a certain function, rather than understanding the liberal problematic of the state as an art of *government* intended to limit the power of the *state*. Foucault traced the development of political thinking from its early concern for the just and good life through the phase associated with Machiavelli, which concentrated on the prince's power, to its development as the theory of raison d'etat, wherein the state was freed from both the larger ethical order *and* the prince's power to become an end in itself. This represented a new principle of political rationality—bio-power—based upon extending the power of the state through a range of disciplinary technologies that act upon our bodies (through government health policies, laws, and educational programs designed to direct or restrict reproductive and sexual activities, incarceration, and other forms of punishment that act through the body, and so on) to create docile and useful subjects. Both Foucault and Derrida, returning to Kant's cosmopolitical writings, have addressed themselves to the prospect for global governance. Derrida has talked about both deepening democracy and—entertaining developments of new technologies—a "democracy to come."

Finally, if there is one key element that distinguishes poststructuralism it is the notion of *difference*. This strong emphasis on difference comes from Nietzsche, Saussure, and Heidegger. As noted above, in *Nietzsche and Philosophy*, Deleuze interprets Nietzsche's philosophy according to the principle of difference and advances this interpretation as an attack upon the Hegelian dialectic. Derrida's notion of difference, on the other hand, can be traced back to two main sources: Saussure's insight that linguistic systems are constituted through difference, and the Heideggerian notion of difference. From the first mention of the notion of difference in this tradition (in 1959) to its development as *différance* takes nearly a decade.

Différance, as Derrida remarks, is both the common root of all the positional concepts marking our language and the condition for all signification, referring not only to the "movement that consists in deferring by means of delay, delegation, reprieve, referral, detour, postponement, reserving," but also and finally to "the unfolding of difference," of the ontico-ontological difference, which Heidegger named as the difference between Being (the abstract property) and beings (the existence of particular people and things) (1981: 8–9). As such, *différance* is seen as plotting the linguistic limits of the subject. As we have already seen in this chapter, Derrida questions the "structurality of structure" or the notion of a "center." His point is that the history of the very concept of structure is tied up with the metaphysics of the human subject whose being is determined as an affirmative presence (for example, a being with a fixed "human nature"). But the "decentering" of structure and of the *sovereign* subject is a way of becoming suspicious of this humanist conception of the human subject; such fixed characteristics are viewed not as givens but as ways of emphasizing and valorizing particular human traits as over and above other equally "human" qualities that are devalued by decentering. In the field of education, for example, the history of conceiving the human subject as a *conscious, rational, autonomous* being—a legacy of the Cartesian-Kantian tradition—has played a significant role in constructing particular moral and cognitive accounts of "pupils," "students," and "learners" that highlight certain educational purposes while suppressing others.

Lyotard, by contrast, invents the concept of the *différend*, "a case of conflict, between (at least) two parties, that cannot be equitably resolved for lack of a rule of judgment applicable to both arguments" (1988: xi). He suggests that this gap of possible consensus, this incommensurability or inexpressibility of a surplus of meaning, establishes the very condition for the existence of all discourse: "a universal rule of judgment between heterogeneous genre is lacking in general" (1988: xi), or again, "there is no genre whose hegemony over others would be just" (1988: 158). Lyotard's *différend* is important not only in terms of questioning liberal accounts of inquiry, democracy, or education based on consensus and agreement (as in Habermas's notion of the ideal communication society), but also for demonstrating that such accounts sometimes are built upon *exclusions* that cannot be talked about within the available, privileged vocabulary. By contrast, Lyotard argues we must first detect these unspoken/unspeakable *différends* (a cognitive task) and bear witness to them (an ethical task); this often entails questioning the available vocabulary (a political task).

These poststructuralist notions of difference, often expressed through the term "anti-essentialism," have been more recently developed in relation to gender and ethnicity: The American feminist philosopher Iris Marion Young (1991) writes of *Justice and the Politics of Difference* and the Afro-American philosopher, Cornel West (1993) speaks of "The New Cultural Politics of Difference." Henry Giroux and Elizabeth Ellsworth, among others, have carried these questions of difference and cultural or identity politics into the realm of education.

We have used part of Lyotard's definition of the "postmodern condition" to characterize this feature of poststructuralism, a suspicion of transcendental arguments and viewpoints, combined with the rejection of canonical descriptions and final vocabularies. In particular, an "incredulity toward metanarratives" refers to the question of legitimation in the modern age, where particular grand narratives have been advanced as part of the exercise of state power (for example, in the present context of 2003, principles of national security and sovereignty). In Lyotard's view, there is no neutral master discourse that can reproduce the speculative unity of knowledge or adjudicate between competing views, claims, or discourses without imposing a set of interests of its own.

The last feature of this chapter we take from Foucault's analytics of power: the diagnosis of "power/knowledge" and the analysis of technologies of domination. For Foucault, power is productive; it is dispersed throughout the social system, and it is intimately related to knowledge. Power is productive because it is not simply repressive; it also creates new knowledge (which may also liberate). It is dispersed rather than located in any one center, like the state. It is part of the constellation "power/knowledge," which means that knowledge, in the sense of discursive practices, is generated through the exercise of power in the control of the body. Foucault develops this thesis about the interrelations of power and knowledge through his genealogical study of the development of modern institutions such as the prison and the school, and the corresponding emergence of the social sciences that helped devise new methods and vocabularies of social control in their relation to, and regulation of, such institutions. As we see later in this book, this analysis of the social and institutional effects of knowledge, and the reflexive critique of ostensibly neutral research methods and vocabularies, places a serious constraint on the exercise of educational research—poststructuralism wants to ask questions beyond traditional issues of truth, objectivity, or "useful knowledge."

CONCLUSION

We have argued that while there are both historical and theoretical overlaps and "family resemblances" between postmodernism and poststructuralism, it is possible to distinguish between the two movements in terms of their respective intellectual genealogies and their theoretical trajectories and applications. One important set of theoretical and historical differences can be seen most easily by recognizing the differences between their *theoretical objects of study*—modernism, in the first case, and structuralism, in the second.

We also have argued that the theoretical development of French structuralism during the late 1950s and 1960s led to an institutionalization of a transdisciplinary "mega-paradigm," founded upon the linguistic model, that helped to integrate the humanities and the social sciences, but did so in an overly optimistic and *scientistic* conception. In this sense it was part of the broader "linguistic turn" taken by Western philosophy but also reflected a strongly formalist turn that, in the hands of Saussure, Jakobson, and others following them, radically undermined both the humanistic construction of the subject as an autonomous, free, and creative or expressive individual, and the model of the text and textual interpretation based upon it—a model that assumed clear and fathomable intentions that determined meaning.

To a large extent poststructuralist thought shared with this immediate predecessor—structuralism—a radical questioning of the problematic of the humanist subject. Deriving its inspiration from Nietzsche and Heidegger, and conditioned by the densely intellectual Parisian environment of the postwar years, it provided a philosophical response to the scientistic pretensions and totalizing nature of structuralism, which had been elevated to the status of a universally valid theory for understanding language, thought, society, culture, economy, and indeed, all aspects of the human enterprise. The waning of confidence in the scientific ambitions of structuralism that took place after 1968 issued in a new critical pluralism that decentered the master discourse of structuralism, promoting at the same time an emphasis on the plurality of interpretation through the concepts of *play, indeterminacy,* and *différance.* Poststructuralism moved decisively away from all forms of foundationalism.

When discussing poststructuralism, it is important to recognize it as a movement (perhaps construed in the musical sense of the term)—as a complex skein that intertwines many different strands and also conceals important differences among the thinkers identified as poststructuralist. We have tried to give some flavor here to the range of quite different views all clustered under this heading. Moreover, poststructuralism as a movement is in its third or fourth generation. Foucault, Deleuze, and Lyotard are now dead. Derrida has carried the movement, originating in France, across the Atlantic, first and most obviously to American departments of literature. Foucault and Lyotard had visiting professorships at one time or another in various American universities. The theoretical effects of their work are clearly evident in a variety of disciplines, including philosophy, sociology, politics, and cultural studies. If poststructuralism in its first and second generation might be conceived as largely a French affair, it is no longer the case: third- and fourth-generation poststructuralists—feminists, postcolonialists, psychoanalysts, neo-Foucauldians, Deleuzeans, Derrideans—in the English-speaking world, and increasingly in Third World nations, are seeking to both develop and apply the thought of earlier poststructuralists in a series of experiments and theoretical mutations. Educational thought is one of the areas in which these trends have had a significant impact—a point we illustrate with examples throughout this book. In the next two chapters, we trace the specific influence of poststructuralist thought on the aims and the methods of educational research.

REFERENCES

Abrams, M. H. 1981. *Glossary of Literary Terms.* New York: Holt, Rinehart and Winston.

Culler, J. 1976. *Saussure.* Hassocks, Sussex, U.K.: The Harvester Press.

Deleuze, Gilles. [1962] 1983. *Nietzsche and Philosophy.* Translated by H. Tomlinson. New York: Columbia University Press.

——. 1995. *Negotiations, 1972–1990.* Translated by Martin Joughlin. New York: Columbia University Press.

Derrida, Jacques. 1978. "Structure, Sign, and Play in the Discourses of the Human Sciences." Pp. 278–93 in *Writing and Difference*. Translated by Alan Bass. Chicago: University of Chicago Press.

———. 1981. *Positions*. Translated by Alan Bass. Chicago: University of Chicago Press.

Dosse, Francois. 1997. *History of Structuralism*. Vols. 1 and 2. Translated by Deborah Glassman. Minneapolis: University of Minnesota Press.

Easthope, Anthony. 1988. *British Post-Structuralism since 1968*. New York: Routledge.

Ermarth, E. D. 1996. "Postmodernism." Pp. 587–90 in *Routledge Encyclopedia of Philosophy*. Edited by E. Craig. New York: Routledge.

Foucault. 1983. "The Subject and Power." Pp. in 208–26 in H. Dreyfus and P. Rabinow. *Michel Foucault: Beyond Structuralism and Hermeneutics*. 2d ed. Chicago: Chicago University Press.

———. 1996. "How Much Does It Cost To Tell the Truth?" In *Foucault Live: Interviews 1966–84*. Edited by S. Lotringer, translated by J. Johnson. New York: Semiotext(e).

———. 1991. *Remarks on Marx: Conversations with Duccio Trombadori*. Translated by R. Goldstein and J. Cascaito. New York: Semiotext(e).

Frank, Manfred. 1988. *What Is Neo-Structuralism?* Translated by Sabine Wilke and Richard Gray, foreword by Martin Schwab. Minneapolis: University of Minnesota Press.

Gadet, F. 1989. *Saussure and Contemporary Culture*. Translated by G. Elliot. London: Hutchinson.

Greenberg, C. 1973. "Modernist Painting." Pp. 596–600 in *The New Art*. Edited by G. Battock. New York: Dutton.

Gutting, G. 1998a. "Post-Structuralism." Pp. 596–600 in *Routledge Encyclopedia of Philosophy*. Edited by E. Craig. New York: Routledge.

———. 1998b "Post-Structuralism in the Social Sciences." Pp. 600–604 in *Routledge Encyclopedia of Philosophy*. Edited by E. Craig. New York: Routledge.

Harland, Richard. 1987. *Superstructuralism: The Philosophy of Structuralism and Post-Structuralism*. London and New York: Methuen.

———. 1993. *Beyond Superstructuralism: The Syntagmatic Side of Language*. New York: Routledge.

Heidegger, Martin. [1961] 1991. *Nietzsche*. 2 vols. Translated by David Krell. San Francisco: Harper.

Hengehold, L. 1998. "Subject, Postmodern Critique of The." Pp. 196–201 in *Routledge Encyclopedia of Philosophy*. Edited by E. Craig. New York: Routledge.

Jakobson, Roman. 1973. *Main Trends in the Science of Language*. London: Allen & Unwin.

Lévi-Strauss, Claude. [1958] 1968. *Structural Anthropology*. London: Allen & Unwin.

Lilly, R. 1998. "Postmodernism and Political Philosophy." Pp. 590–96. In *Routledge Encyclopedia of Philosophy*. Edited by E. Craig. New York: Routledge.

Lyotard, Jean-François. 1988. *The Différend: Phrases in Dispute*. Translated by Georges Van Den Abbeele. Minneapolis: University of Minnesota Press.

———. [1979] 1984. *The Postmodern Condition: A Report on Knowledge*. Translated by Geoff Bennington and Brian Massumi with a foreword by Fredric Jameson. Minneapolis: University of Minnesota Press.

——. 1992. *The Postmodern Explained to Children: Correspondence 1982–1985.* Sydney: Power Publications.

Macksey, Richard, and Eugenio Donato, eds. 1970. *The Structuralist Controversy: The Languages of Criticism and the Sciences of Man.* Baltimore: Johns Hopkins Press.

Peters, Michael A. 1995. *Education and the Postmodern Condition.* Foreword by Jean-François Lyotard. Westport, Conn., and London: Bergin & Garvey.

——. 1996. *Poststructuralism, Politics and Education,* Westport, Conn., and London: Bergin & Garvey.

——. 1998. "Introduction: Naming the Multiple." In *Naming the Multiple: Poststructuralism and Education.* Edited by M. Peters. Westport, Conn., and London: Bergin & Garvey.

——, ed. 2002. *Heidegger, Education, and Modernity.* Lanham, Md.: Rowman & Littlefield.

Piaget, Jean. [1968] 1971. *Structuralism.* New York: Routledge & Kegan Paul.

Poster, Mark. 1989. *Critical Theory and Poststructuralism: In Search of a Context.* Ithaca, N.Y.: Cornell University Press.

Saussure, Ferdinand. [1916] 1974. *Course in General Linguistics.* Edited by Charles Bally and Albert Sechehaye with Albert Reidlinger, translated by Wade Baskin. London: Fontana.

Schrift, Alan. 1995. *Nietzsche's French Legacy: A Genealogy of Poststructuralism.* New York: Routledge.

——. 1996. "Poststructuralism." Pp. 452–53 in *The Encyclopedia of Philosophy, Supplement.* Edited by D. Borchert. New York: Macmillan, Simon & Schuster.

Selden, Raman, ed. 1995. *The Cambridge History of Literary Criticism: From Formalism to Poststructuralism.* Vol. 8. Cambridge: Cambridge University Press.

Silverman, H. J. 1996. "Modernism and Postmodernism." Pp. 353–54 in *The Encyclopedia of Philosophy, Supplement.* Edited by D. Borchert. New York: Macmillan, Simon & Schuster.

Sturrock, John. 1986. *Structuralism.* London: Paladin.

Waugh, Linda, R., and Monique Monville-Burston. 1990. *On Language: Roman Jakobson.* Cambridge, Mass.: Harvard University Press.

West, Cornel. 1992. "The New Cultural Politics of Difference." In *Keeping Faith: Philosophy and Race in America.* New York: Routledge.

Young, I. M. 1991. *Justice and the Politics of Difference.* Princeton, N.J.: Princeton University Press.

2

Poststructuralism and the Aims of Educational Research

We ourselves are not only the beings, that reason but also one of the objects, concerning which we reason.

David Hume, *A Treatise of Human Nature*, xix

The very concept of human nature [in the eighteenth century] and the way in which it functioned, precluded a classical science of man.

Michel Foucault, *The Order of Things*, 309

COMPETING CONCEPTIONS OF SOCIAL SCIENCE

At the end of the last chapter we distinguished some of the main characteristics—the theoretical tendencies and innovations—of poststructuralism. The aims of poststructuralist educational research are strongly related to these characteristics, yet it is difficult to talk of "aims" in relation to poststructuralism because it is not possible, strictly speaking, to ascribe specific aims to a cultural moment that is more like a complex variety of thought or a movement (in the musical sense) than a school, a doctrine, or body of theory. "Aims," similar to "purposes" or "goals," imply some level of intentionality. It is difficult to speak of intentionality (the capacity to make intentions) without at the same time referring to an individual (or a group that acts collectively like an individual). We should, therefore, be careful not to homogenize the thought of many contemporary thinkers—who often disagree with one another—into one set of theoretical practices that can be easily packaged into a methodology to be adopted by researchers in the field of education who call themselves "poststructuralist." While we shall use the term "aims" in relation to poststructuralism, we do so with this caveat.

Certainly, the central aim of research of any sort is to produce knowledge; but what does it mean to produce knowledge? One of the main aims of poststructuralism is to provide a *genealogy* of social phenomena in order to analyze power/knowledge configurations. It could be argued that educational researchers who seek to use poststructuralist perspectives must first, therefore, develop a critical self-understanding of the historical conditions of the formation and genealogy of their own discipline. Accordingly, we begin this chapter with a brief discussion of some different views of "science" (and "research") as they have been part of the historical development of the human or social sciences (including educational research). Often, these notions are taken for granted, viewed as "natural," or seen as uncontested or uncontestable and, therefore, not open to question. Yet the question of the aims of science and research can only be answered if we first investigate what view of science or research we are embracing. In other words, the question of aims is strongly related to an understanding of contested views of "science," especially as they apply to social or human affairs. In this chapter we discuss in this regard two influential poststructuralist views of scientific rationality: Michel Foucault's genealogy of the human sciences, and Jean-François Lyotard's critique of what he calls "capitalist technoscience." Toward the end of the chapter we will be better able to approach the question of the aims of educational research that bases itself upon poststructuralist philosophy.

The term "science" and its more recent cousin, "research," are historically recent notions. *Scientia* was the term used in the Latin culture of late medieval Europe simply to mean "systematic knowledge." It was in the eighteenth century that two clearly different approaches (or epistemologies) developed in relation to the attainment of scientific knowledge and to human beings: René Descartes' rationalism and John Locke's empiricism. Roughly speaking, we might say that Descartes' rationalism was based upon the belief that reason (the powers of the intellect), rather than sense experience, is the most reliable source of knowledge—as opposed to Locke's empiricism, which maintained that sense experience is the only reliable source of knowledge. The standard distinction between the *rationalists* (Descartes, Spinoza, Leibniz) and the *empiricists* (Locke, Berkeley, Hume), despite its historical inaccuracies and stereotyping, has traditionally played a major role in framing our understanding of the history of philosophy of science, and played a significant role in our understanding of the emergence of the social sciences. Thus, in the eighteenth century, empiricist Enlightenment philosophers such as Locke and Hume sought to extend the methods of natural sciences to the so-called moral sciences. Human nature was seen as constant, uniform, and predictable—and therefore a suitable prospect for the application of science, the search for laws or regularities. David Hume is probably the best example of an empiricist philosopher who proposed a "science of man." By emulating the methods of the newly successful natural sciences, based on Francis Bacon's "experimentalism" and Isaac Newton's analytical method, Hume thought not only that knowledge of human beings was possible, but that progress toward establishing a general, unified, scientific *theory of human nature* was simply a matter of time.

The positivist tradition of thought, dating from the social theories of St. Simon and Auguste Comte, also embraces a *naturalist* thesis—that is, the argument that there is only one scientific method common to all the sciences, whether they be natural or social/human/moral. This tradition, combined with empiricism in the early-twentieth century (under the name "logical empiricism" or "logical positivism"), became the mainstream Anglo-American view of science and the dominant paradigm in the social sciences and educational research. (For a general account of developments in philosophy of science, see Chalmers, 1990; for a feminist account see Harding, 1991).

We can characterize positivism, in general terms, by the following assumptions:

- philosophy should be scientific
- metaphysics is nonsense
- there is a universal and a priori scientific method
- the main task of philosophy is to analyze that method
- there is an objective, independent reality we call the world
- truth is correspondence to reality
- scientists discover truth as spectators of a world, which is essentially a given
- there is a methodological unity of the sciences
- reductionism, in principle, is possible and desirable
- facts can be unambiguously distinguished from values
- theoretical statements should be translatable into statements about observation (the observation/theory distinction).

In addition, in the social sciences, positivism has tended to accept a series of other assumptions or doctrines. For instance, it has tended to emphasize quantitative data and rigorous experimental or quasi-experimental methods over forms of qualitative and especially ethnographic research. It has also often been associated with the doctrines of behaviorism and operationalism. The social sciences, under positivism, have tended to adopt the principles of methodological individualism, the belief that for purposes of analysis only individuals count.

At the same time, positivist social science has entertained a deep skepticism about the scientific status of interpretation, meaning, and the understanding of social practices, exhibiting a bias in favor of conceptual analysis in social science rather than the actual practice of social research. (For an extended critique of these positivist assumptions, see D. C. Phillips and Nicholas C. Burbules, *Postpositivism and Educational Research* [Lanham, Md.: Rowman & Littlefield, 2000], another book in this series.)

By contrast to both empiricism and positivism, historically we can talk of a competing conception of the social/human sciences. Emerging in Germany in the mid-nineteenth century, the term *Geisteswissenschaften* was an attempt to translate John Stuart Mill's notion of "the moral sciences." On this view—developed and promoted by Wilhelm Dilthey, Wilhelm Windelband, and Heinrich Rickert—science (*Wissenschaft*) applies to all disciplined and systematic research that aims at knowledge. It also holds that it is possible to distinguish between its two branches: the natural sciences (*Naturwissenschaften*) and the human sciences (*Geisteswissenschaften*). The latter—the *Geisteswissenschaften*—draw upon the notion of *Geist*, which can be translated as "spirit" or "mind," and in this context refer to "culture" or the cultural realm. Sometimes the German word *Kulturwissenschaften* is used as a substitute. Both are seen as exhibiting a methodological difference from the natural sciences in that cultural products or manifestations can only be grasped through *Verstehen* (or "understanding"), as opposed to *Erklärung* (or "explanation") in the natural sciences. The former relies on "understanding" of the meaning of human action by reference to human intentions; the latter seeks "explanation" of natural phenomena and aims at the establishment of causal laws. The former falls under the *ideographic* (or individualizing) sciences, the latter, under the *monothetic* (or generalizing) sciences.

In crude terms, and for the purpose of this chapter, it is useful to distinguish between an Anglo-American view of the social sciences that generally treats social phenomena in the same way as natural phenomena, and a European/Continental view of the human sciences that generally treats social phenomena in terms of the linguistic and symbolic representation of meaning and value. The various forms of *phenomenological*, *existential*, and *hermeneutical* inquiry belong to this broad tradition.

By contrast, structuralism both differs from positivism and the *Geisteswissenschaften* and shares certain elements with them. It shares with positivism, in general, its faith in science and scientific progress as well as in formalization and analytical rigor; it assumes that structuralist methodology can be usefully applied to both natural and social sciences. It differs with positivism in insisting upon the concept of wholeness, of the *system*, and of the importance of relations of constituent elements that comprise structures or systems; to this extent it stands against the analytical, reductionistic procedures of positivism and its linear conception of causality. With the human sciences (the *Geisteswissenschaften*) structuralism shares the emphasis upon linguistic methods and the symbolic representation of value, and even of human intentions and cultural productions—though it differs with the *Geisteswissenschaften* in recognizing the means for accessing such meaning. If there is meaning or value, structuralism maintains, it exists not as a result of the individual, knowing subject, construed as the author of its own semantic intentions and historical agency, but rather by virtue of a set of rules or conventions that structure language, culture, and institutions. To that extent, as we saw in the preceding chapter, structuralism can be seen as a cultural moment of the broader movement of European formalism, part of the formal experimentalism in method that gave birth simultaneously to structuralist linguistics and poetics, and to European futurism—a nascent project of formalization shared widely by developments in mathematics, logic, architecture, the physical sciences, and philosophy.

MICHEL FOUCAULT AND THE HISTORY OF THE HUMAN SCIENCES

The history of the human sciences begins with the Renaissance and the attempts by Renaissance scholars to study and explain the human subject, the self. This has often been referred to as "humanism" and described in terms of a philosophical and literary movement that treats as central the questions of human values and of what it means to be human. Michel Foucault, writing in *The Order of Things*, underscores the importance of an interest in the study of "man" to humanism and the human sciences when he argues that "man is only a recent invention, a figure not yet two centuries old, a new wrinkle in our knowledge, and that he will disappear again as soon as that knowledge has discovered a new form" (1973: xxiii). Foucault also returns to this theme at the end of the book:

> Man is neither the oldest nor the most constant problem that has been posed for human knowledge. Taking a relatively short sample within a restricted geographical area—European culture since the sixteenth century—one can be certain that man is a recent invention within it. . . . As the archaeology of our thought easily shows, man is an invention of recent date. And perhaps one nearing its end. (1973: 387)

Without doubt, humanism in its various forms, and particularly during its nascent development in the Renaissance, profoundly influenced Western conceptions of social science and, more directly, of education and pedagogy. One might say that modern Western traditions of pedagogy and education were inaugurated and shaped by Renaissance humanism, not only in terms of its adoption of the model of Latin letters, the revival of classical literature, and the reproduction of its literary forms as the basis for the "new learning," but also, in a more deeply cultural sense, in terms of the underlying philosophical assumptions constituting notions of human nature and human inquiry, and the relations of human beings to the natural world. Contemporary educational ideas and values such as moral perfectibility, social progress, and personal autonomy are the direct outgrowth of this humanist tradition.

Humanism came to be defined as a new vision of "man" and a new philosophy. Art historians of the first half of the twentieth century saw a new emphasis in painting on worldly rather than divine subjects, an emphasis that accentuated the dignity of man and the centrality of human values, especially rationality and freedom, together with tolerance and an acceptance of human limitations. By the mid-twentieth century historians had redefined humanism as educational reform—in the sense that humanism begins in the study of *humanitas*, the humanities or humane arts. Paul Oskar Kristeller, for instance, defines humanism as a return to the classics as texts, an antischolastic emphasis on rhetoric rather than logic, and the study of moral philosophy (understood as a marriage of Christianity and classical thought), history, and poetry rather than theology. He writes:

> Humanism was understood . . . as that broad concern with the study and imitation of classical antiquity which was characteristic of the period and found its expression in scholarship and education. . . . The modern term "humanism" . . . was derived from the term "humanist" coined in the late fifteenth century to designate a teacher and student of the humanities or *studia humanitatis*. The word "humanity" and its derivatives were associated with a "liberal" education by several Roman writers, especially Cicero and Gellius. The term was revived by Petrarch, Salutati and others in the fourteenth century, and by the middle of the fifteenth century came to stand for a well-defined cycle of studies, called *studia humanitatis*, which included *grammatica*, *rhetorica*, *poetica*, *historia* and *philosophia moralis*. (1988: 113)

The restoration of classical Latin as a living language reformed Medieval Latin (its spelling, prosody, punctuation, vocabulary, phraseology, and syntax), leading to the production of textbooks of grammar, detailed commentaries, word indexes, and thesauri. Humanist scholars also claimed the importance of eloquence and its inseparability from wisdom as central to the ideal of the educated man, and produced works on rhetoric of both a theoretical and practical nature. The favored genres were the oration and the letter, although humanist prose composition also involved histories, philosophical writings, poetry, and literary criticism. In all the variety of their literary productions what was new was "the tendency to take seriously their own personal feelings and experiences, opinions, and preferences" (Kristeller, 1988: 126), an emphasis on subjectivity not typical of ancient literature.

Humanism, then, generally came to represent the set of beliefs based upon the central idea that individual human beings are the fundamental source of value and have the ability to understand and control the natural world through the exercise of their own rational faculties. The centrality of the human will is perhaps most notably expressed in Giovanni Pico della Mirandola's *Oration on the Dignity of Man*, first published in 1486. The emphasis on the human will and upon "becoming what we will" became immensely influential in the sixteenth and seventeenth centuries. In terms of the Enlightenment, humanism "insisted on man's essential autonomy: man is responsible to himself, to his own rational interests, to his self-development and by an inescapable extension, to the welfare of his fellow man" (Gay, 1970: 398). This will to self-development has come to be manifested not only in education proper, but also in the growth of the "human sciences" by which we seek to understand ourselves and gain a knowledge of social affairs that will allow rational social planning and reform.

Foucault was strongly influenced by Martin Heidegger who, in "Letter on Humanism," famously reexamined the humanity of man only to argue: "It lies in his essence" (1996: 224). Heidegger takes us through a brief genealogy of the concept "humanism," beginning with the *first* humanism that is in essence Roman:

> *Humanitas*, explicitly so called, was first considered and striven for in the age of the Roman Republic. *Homo humanas* was opposed to *homo barbarus*. *Homo humanas* here means the Romans, who exalted and honored Roman *virtus* through the "embodiment" of the *paideia* [education] taken over from the Greeks. These were the Greeks of the Hellenistic age, whose culture was acquired in the schools of philosophy. It was concerned with *erditio et institutio in bonas artes* [scholarship and training in good conduct]. *Paideia* thus understood was translated as humanities. The genuine *romanitas of homo romanus* consisted in such *humanitas*. We encounter the first humanism in Rome: it therefore remains in essence a specifically Roman phenomenon, which emerges from the encounter of Roman civilization with the culture of late Greek civilization. (1996: 224)

One of his startling conclusions is stated in the following passage:

> Every humanism is either grounded in metaphysics or is itself made to be the ground of one. Every determination of the essence of man that already presupposes an interpretation of beings without asking about the truth of Being, whether knowingly or not, is metaphysical. (1996: 225–26)

The key assumption of humanist thought, which is often unreflective of its own history and uncritical of its governing principles, is the notion that the self is a stable, coherent, and knowable entity. In liberal political thought dating from Immanuel Kant, the self is attributed "rights" and considered a conscious, rational, autonomous agent. This view of the self as a person with "inalienable rights" is then granted an abstract and universal status. Karl Marx criticized this view as ideological when he wrote: "none of the so-called rights of man goes beyond egoistic man. . . . An individual withdrawn behind his private interests and whims and separated from the community" (1977: 54). Eugene Kamenka makes a similar point as both Foucault and Marx when he provides a brief history of the concept of rights and the ways in which rights rest upon the culture-bound notion of the individual person:

> The concept of human rights . . . sees society as an association of individuals, as founded—logically or historically—on a contract between them, and it elevates the individual human person and his freedom and happiness to be the goal and end of all human association. In the vast majority of human societies, in time and space, until very recently such a view of human society would have been hotly contested; indeed, most cultures and languages would not have had the words in which to express it plausibly. (1978: 15)

Therefore, humanism, as a movement, especially in its Enlightenment guise, begins to construct a very powerful picture of the self as a knowing subject: The self both knows itself and the world through reason, and reason or rationality is posited as the highest form of human functioning. This view of the rational self then becomes the basis for a mode of knowing that is considered "scientific" in the sense that it can provide truths about the world. Such knowledge produced by science is deemed to be both "true" and "objective." This kind of knowledge—scientific knowledge produced by the rational knowing self—is believed to lead to progress, improvement, and moral perfectibility in human affairs. The human sciences can be seen in one sense as a development out of humanist thought based upon the sovereignty of the human subject or the self. To what extent, we must ask, do the existing paradigms of educational research embody aspects of humanism? Think of liberal humanism and existentialist and humanist Marxism as research approaches in education. These approaches are characterized by a feature Sartre described in terms of "existence precedes essence," meaning that humanism concerns self-development or one's life as a historical project shaped through the moral choices one makes rather than as a given essence that is simply bought to fruition through appropriate socialization or education. Humanist research approaches in education—for example, in life-history analysis, early Freirean literacy studies, liberal political economy of education—thus tend to emphasize the moral and political agency of the subject, which often assumes the subject as rational, autonomous, and self-transparent.

Foucault progressively reformulated this project on humanism into one that analyzed the *various* modes through which human beings have been constituted in Western culture as both subjects and objects of knowledge. In *The Order of Things* (1973), subtitled *An Archaeology of The Human Sciences*, and *The Archaeology of Knowledge* ([1977] 1992) Foucault investigates the historical conditions of possibility for the formation of the human sciences. The former text investigates humanism or the human sciences in terms of the conditions of possibility for man to emerge as an object of knowledge, focusing upon the discursive rules of formation structuring different modes of thought. Foucault's study reveals that the origin of modern thought—of the human sciences—is not found in the gradual and progressive transformation of a form of thought from earlier forms, but rather as a radical mutation or break with the classical.

In the classical *episteme* (a system of epistemological relations that unites discourses at a certain period)—roughly from the mid-seventeenth century to the beginning of the nineteenth century—knowledge was ordered in terms of representation: a general method worked to classify representations in the form of a table of differences that mirrored the order of things in the world. In other words, representation was the dominant motif that provided the epistemological unity for a general method typifying all discourses. Foucault investigates this thesis by reference to the discursive formation of language (general grammar), nature (natural history), and the science of wealth (economics). Within the classical *episteme* there is no place for "man" as an object of knowledge and, therefore, no possibility for the development of a "science of man."

The shift to the modern *episteme* is marked precisely by a configuration of knowledge centered on the figure of man as both subject and object of knowledge. The difficulties of the human sciences, particularly their uncertainty *as* "sciences"—despite the increasing formalization and even mathematization of their methods—is due to this ambiguous position, this doubleness and complexity of man as both subject and object, which is the knowledge configuration of the modern *episteme* (Foucault, 1973: 34). The history of the human sciences is a history of the progressive adoption of one dominant analytical model after another, taken from the empirical sciences of philology, biology, and economics, and a shift away from function to meaning and signification. Alongside this shift, Foucault notes a related movement away from an emphasis on processes accessible to consciousness to an emphasis upon the rules or norms that govern structures or systems. The human sciences, nevertheless, remain within the ambit of representation, forced to attend to the meanings we give things rather than analyzing the things themselves.

It could be argued that Foucault, in providing this historical narrative, is simply recapitulating his own experience, at least insofar as he grants (post)structuralism the apex of present development in the ongoing story of a true human science, substituting the science of language for the science of man. With Foucault, the poststructuralist educational researcher might ask:

• What are the various modes in Western culture (and in other cultures) through which children and adults have been constituted as knowing, learning, and educated subjects?
• What are the various ways children and adults have been constituted as subjects of educational research, of pedagogy, and of theories of human development?
• What are the interrelations between various forms of knowledge and power in education and educational research?
• In educational institutions *how* is power exercised?
• To what extent has educational research constructed its own history as one of steady progress toward greater objectivity and laws concerning human development and learning?

Foucault was among the first, now almost thirty years ago, to raise questions concerning the unities of discourse and of disciplines and to interrogate the notion of "disciplinarity" itself. His "archaeology" as the "epistemological mutation of history" is a form of structuralism, but one that is decentered through the operation of Nietzschean genealogy, that eschews the search for origins and foundations. Foucault was forever questioning and progressively refining his own project as one that concerned the problematic of the subject, and his archaeology of knowledge is also defined in these terms. As he says, "Making historical analysis the discourse of the continuous and making human consciousness the original subject of all historical development and action are two sides of the same system of thought" (12). It is no wonder then that when he assumed his chair at the prestigious Collége de France in 1970 at the age of forty-four, he called his chair "The History of Systems of Thought." "Systems of thought," he suggested, "are the forms in which, during a given time, knowledges individualize, achieve an equilibrium, and enter into communication." As Paul Rabinow explains, Foucault divided his work on the history of systems of thought into three interrelated parts: the "reexamination of knowledge, the conditions of knowledge, and the knowing subject" (1997: xi). The discursive formation and transformation of knowledge (and its disciplinary forms) is constituted by rules that characterize "its existence, its operation, and its history" (Foucault, 1997: 7).

Foucault first takes the given disciplinary unities and asks what formally unites them as fields specified in space and individualized in time. By suspending the naturalness of these accepted unities it is possible to describe or define other unities. *The Archaeology of Knowledge* is Foucault's attempt to describe the relations between statements that constitute a field of discourse in terms of the objects to which they refer, the style they manifest, the system of concepts they establish, and the themes they identify. In chapter 6, "Science and Knowledge" Foucault inquires:

> If one calls "disciplines" groups of statements that borrow their organization from scientific models, which tend to coherence and demonstrativity, which are accepted, institutionalized, transmitted, and sometimes taught as sciences, could one not say that archaeology describes disciplines that are not really sciences, while epistemology describes sciences that have been formed on the basis of (or in spite of) existing disciplines? (1992: 178)

Archaeology defines the rules of formation of a group of statements; it does not describe disciplines. Disciplines may serve as starting points for the description of "positivities," but "they do not fix it limits" or "impose definitive divisions upon it" (1992: 179). By "positivities" Foucault means what characterizes the unity of a discourse through time—a historical a priori that, as a form of positivity, defines "a field in which formal identities, thematic continuities, translations of concepts, and polemical interchanges may be deployed" (1992: 127). In short, positivities do not characterize forms of knowledge. In liberal economic approaches to education, these positivities may be a set of unexamined beliefs about the status of the sovereign subject and its ability to make choices that reflect individuality, rationality, and self-interest—the characteristics of *homo economicus*.

Yet "archaeology" was still too static an approach and, while different from structuralism per se, it bore all its traces. The conception of disciplines as "structures" carried with it the criticisms of structuralism itself. The notion of disciplines as knowledge "structures" or forms assumed a fixed origin, or center, that freezes the play of difference and meaning in a totalizing gesture around a transcendental subject, which itself is construed as the fount of all meaning, knowledge, and moral action. As we discussed in the preceding chapter, Foucault went to great pains to dissociate himself from structuralism; eventually his own methods underwent a trajectory that carried him away from "archaeology" toward a genealogical approach strongly indebted to Nietzsche's *Genealogy of Morals* ([1887] 1956) and to Nietzsche's associated concept of the will to power (see Mahon, 1992; Peters, 1996, 1997). Foucault discusses the will to power in one of the Collége course summaries entitled "The Will to

Knowledge" where he suggests that it is possible to analyze systems of thought at the level of *discursive practices*:

> Discursive practices are characterized by the demarcation of a field of objects, by the definition of a legitimate perspective for a subject of knowledge, by the setting of norms for elaborating concepts and theories. Hence, each of them presupposes a play of prescriptions that governs exclusions and selections. (1997: 11)

This approach differs from structuralism in that it does not emphasize the abstract synchrony and interrelatedness of the system at the expense of diachrony or historical dynamism. At the same time, Foucault shies away from proposing any laws of historical development or transformation with a built-in telos or historical movement toward particular ends (such as the capitalist dream of the fully driven consumer society or the withering of the state and the attainment of formal equality in socialism). All we have are practices shaped differently in different historical eras, and sets of practices (both discursive and institutional) that come to characterize a particular *episteme*.

Principles of exclusion and selection do not refer to a historical or transcendental subject, Foucault argues, but rather "to an anonymous and polymorphous will to knowledge" referencing his remark to Nietzsche's *The Gay Science*, which he describes as presenting "a model of a fundamentally interested knowledge, produced as an event of the will and determining the effect of truth through falsification" (1974: 14). Foucault coins the term "power/knowledge" to capture Nietzsche's insight. For Foucault, knowledge in the human sciences is not disinterested, neutral, objective, or value-free; rather it is inextricably entwined with relations of power. Power produces knowledge and power and knowledge directly imply one another. Power/knowledge relations are not to be analyzed on the model of the subject of knowledge; rather "the subject who knows, the objects to be known and the modalities of knowledge must be regarded as so many effects of these fundamental implications of power/knowledge and their historical transformations. In short it is not the activity of the subject of knowledge that produces a corpus of knowledge, useful or resistant to power, but power/knowledge, the processes and struggles that traverse it and of which it is made up, that determines the forms and possible domains of knowledge" (1991: 27–28).

In their study of Foucault's work, Dreyfus and Rabinow (1982) propose four stages: a Heideggerian stage (typified by his study of madness and reason), an archaeological or quasi-structuralist stage (characterized by *The Archaeology of Knowledge* and *The Order of Things*), a genealogical stage and, finally an ethical stage. The shift from the archaeological to the genealogical stage in Foucault's writings is well represented in *Discipline and Punish*. Like *The History of Sexuality*, *Discipline and Punish* exhibits a Nietzschean genealogical turn focused upon studies of the *will to knowledge* understood as reflecting both discursive and nondiscursive (i.e., institutional) practices and, in particular, the complex relations among power, knowledge, and the body. *Discipline and Punish* is concerned with the body as an object of certain disciplinary technologies of power. Foucault examines the genealogy of forms of punishment and the development of the modern penal institution, discussing in turn torture, punishment, discipline, and the prison.

The section on "discipline," organized into three sections—respectively "docile bodies," "the means of correct training," and "panopticism"—includes an account of the ways the disciplines became general formulas of domination during the seventeenth and eighteenth centuries. Foucault claims that this new political anatomy was evidenced in a multiplicity of often minor processes at different locations that eventually coalesced into a general method. As he says: "They [i.e., disciplinary techniques] were at work in secondary education at a very early date, later in primary schools; they slowly invested the space of the hospital; and, in a few decades, they restructured the military organization" (1991: 138). He talks of disciplinary techniques in terms of "the art of distributions," (the monastic model of enclosure became the most perfect educational regime) and "partitioning" (every individual had his or her own place). Foucault argues "the organization of a serial space was one of the great technical mutations of elementary education" that made it possible to supersede the traditional apprenticeship system where the pupil spends a few minutes with the master while the rest of the group remains idle (1991: 13).

Foucault also details "the control of activities," including the timetable, what he calls "the temporal elaboration of the act" (e.g., marching), and the correlation of the body and gestures (e.g., "good handwriting . . . presupposes a gymnastics"), as well as other aspects. He writes:

> To sum up, it might be said that discipline creates out of the bodies it controls four types of individuality, or rather an individuality that is endowed with four characteristics; it is cellular (by play of spatial distribution), it is organic (by the coding of activities), it is genetic (by the accumulation of time), it is combinatory (by the composition of forces). And, in doing so, it operates four great techniques; it draws up tables; it prescribes movements; it imposes exercises; lastly, in order to obtain the combination of forces, it arranges "tactics." (1991: 167)

He discusses the means of correct training in terms of "hierarchical observation." As he suggests "the school building was to be a mechanism for training . . . a 'pedagogical machine,'" normalizing judgment, and carrying out the examination (1991: 172). The examination "transformed the economy of visibility into the exercise of power," introduced "individuality into the field of documentation," and "surrounded by all its documentary techniques, . . . [made] each individual a 'case'" (1991: 187). Most famously, Foucault discusses "panopticism"—a system of surveillance based on Jeremy Bentham's architectural figure that operates by permitting the relentless and continual observation of inmates at the periphery by officials at the center, without the officials ever being seen.

Discipline and Punish is concerned with the operation of technologies of power and their relations to the emergence of knowledge in the form of new discourses, based around modes of objectification through which human beings became subjects. It is a theme that Foucault develops further in his work on the history of sexuality. Foucault asks: "Why has sexuality been so widely discussed and what has been said about it? What were the effects of power generated by what was said? What are the links between these discourses, these effects of power, and the pleasures that were invested by them? What knowledge was formed as a result of this linkage?" (1979: 11). It is in the course of his inquiries into sexuality and the proliferation of associated discourses that Foucault coins the term "bio-power," considered a kind of anatomo-politics of the human body and control of the population at large.

TOWARD A POLITICAL PHILOSOPHY OF SCIENCE

The standard liberal interpretation of the epistemology of science is based upon the received view of an *external* relationship between knowledge and power. In other words, while power relations can influence what we believe, considerations of power are (or should be) completely irrelevant to which of our beliefs are true and what justifies their status as knowledge. In other words, as Joseph Rouse succinctly expresses it: "Knowledge acquires its epistemological status independent of the operations of power" (1987: 13). According to this general account, knowledge can be applied in order to achieve power, or power may be used to prevent the acquisition of knowledge, or knowledge might liberate us from the effects of power, but power cannot contribute constructively to the achievement of knowledge. This standard view rests on three features ascribed to the notion of power: that it is possessed and exercised by specific agents; that it operates on our representations but not on the world represented; and that it is primarily repressive (Rouse, 1987: 15). Only the second point needs explanation: Our beliefs about the world may be changed or imposed by the exercise of power over us, but the exercise of power cannot guarantee the truth of our beliefs nor change how the world is.

This received view of the relations between knowledge and power has been seriously challenged. For instance, pragmatism challenges the claim that power is external to knowledge by arguing that truth is nothing more than the product of consensus within a community of inquiry (where power relations inevitably exercise some influence). Moreover, if there are no identifiable criteria of truth apart from what we arrive at through the practice of inquiry, then truth criteria themselves are a product of inquiry, and a consideration of power is integral to epistemology. Here, the traditional epistemological problem of distinguishing true from false beliefs is transformed into "the political problem of distinguishing free inquiry from inquiry constrained and distorted by the exercise of power" (Rouse, 1987: 19). Such a view has also been forcefully argued for by Jürgen Habermas, the leading representative of the Frankfurt school. Habermas (1971) develops the thesis that all knowledge is political, by which he means that knowledge is always constituted on the basis of human interests that have developed in and been shaped by social and historical circumstances. He classifies three main types of "knowledge constitutive interests": the technical interest characteristic of the natural sciences produces instrumental (means-end) knowledge aimed at prediction and control; the practical interest of the human sciences produces knowledge governed by the interpretation and understanding of meaning; and the emancipatory interest of the critical social sciences is premised on the values of freedom and rational autonomy.

Furthermore, the so-called new empiricists (Hilary Putnam, Larry Laudan, Mary Hesse) challenge a range of distinctions that supported the received account of the relation between knowledge and power: fact/value, theory/practice, pure/applied, scheme/content. They also reject representational or realist interpretations of scientific theories. In their terms, successful theories have nothing to do with the accuracy of their representations of the world. Successful theories are those that improve our ability to cope with the world, to control it technically; and "technical control, the power to intervene in and manipulate natural events, is not the application of antecedent knowledge but the form scientific knowledge now predominately takes" (Rouse, 1987: 20).

Closer to the themes of this book, a central influence on how poststructuralists think about epistemology has been Foucault's (1980) account of "power/knowledge" as an indissoluble unity. Foucault rethinks the nature of modern power, tracing its development in the birth of the human sciences and associated liberal institutions such as the clinic, the prison, and the school. These new mechanisms of modern power go hand in hand with the birth of the human sciences. Modern power is "productive" rather than simply repressive; it is "capillary" in that it operates in everyday social practices rather than through beliefs; and it is both local and continuous. Truth, knowledge, and belief are a product of the "politics of the discursive regime." There are pluralities of incommensurable discursive regimes that succeed each other historically. Power/knowledge is itself a discursive regime, comprising a matrix of practices that define its own distinctive objects of inquiry, its own truth criteria, its own institutional sanctions, and so on. The term "power/knowledge," as Nancy Fraser notes, "covers in a single concept everything that falls under the two distinct Kuhnian concepts of paradigm and disciplinary matrix but, unlike Kuhn, Foucault gives this complex a political character. Both the use of the term 'power' and, more subtly, that of the term 'regime' convey this political coloration" (1981: 274). Discursive regimes function on the basis of social practices that necessarily involve forms of constraint: the valorization of some statement forms over others; "the institutional licensing of some persons as being entitled to offer knowledge-claims and the concomitant exclusion of others; coercive forms of extracting information from and about certain persons and groups of persons; and so on" (1981: 274).

While Foucault did not apply his insights directly to the natural sciences, others have. For example, Rouse uses Foucault to develop a political philosophy of science. He writes:

> Power relations permeate the most ordinary activities in scientific research. Scientific knowledge arises out of these power relations rather than in opposition to them. Knowledge is power, and power knowledge. Knowledge is embedded in our research practices rather than being fully abstractable in representational theories. Theories are to be understood in their uses, not in their static correspondence . . . with the world. Power as it is produced in science is not the possession of particular agents and does not necessarily serve particular interests. Power relations constitute the world in which we find agents and interests. (1987: 24)

This view of the relations between knowledge and power also underlies Lyotard's account of "the postmodern condition," as we discussed earlier (recall that his book is subtitled "A Report on Knowledge"). Lyotard's primary point of departure in attempting to describe and chart the transition in Western societies to the postindustrial age is its conception of "scientific knowledge." He argues that the leading sciences and technologies—cybernetics, telematics, informatics, and the growth of computer languages—are all significantly *language based*, and together they have transformed the two principal functions of knowledge: research and the transmission of acquired learning. We will now turn to elaborating Lyotard's views on this issue.

LYOTARD AND THE CRITIQUE OF CAPITALIST TECHNOSCIENCE

Lyotard argues that technological and institutional changes have led to a redefined conception of knowledge. Anything in the constituted body of knowledge not translatable into useful information will be abandoned. (A recent policy shift by the present Bush administration to erase all educational research studies from the government ERIC archives that do not reflect their view of credible, useful knowledge is an extreme exemplification of this trend.) Knowledge, in other words, loses its "use-value" apart from its narrowly instrumental outcomes—a process Lyotard terms "performativity." The game of technology, as opposed to science, whose goal is truth, follows the principle of optimal performance (maximizing output, minimizing input); its goal or criterion is efficiency rather than truth or justice. This yields a new hybrid, which Lyotard calls "technoscience." The transformation wrought by new knowledge technologies and markets also changes the way in which learning is acquired and classified. Knowledge becomes exteriorized with respect to the knower; the status of the teacher and learner relation is transformed into a commodity relation of "supplier" and "consumer." As Lyotard argues: "Knowledge is and will be produced in order to be sold, it is and will be consumed in order to be valorized in a new production: in both cases, the goal is exchange" (1984: 4).

Already knowledge has become the principal force of production, severely altering the composition of the workforce in the most developed countries. This is often captured in expressions such as "the New Information Economy" or "knowledge workers." This mercantilization of knowledge is further widening the gap between developed and developing countries, as knowledge becomes one more resource to be hoarded and monopolized for market advantage. But such a proprietary conception of knowledge potentially disrupts the "gift economy" of teacher and student. Moreover, it raises legal and ethical questions for the relationship between the state and information-rich transnational corporations. Clearly, modern societies have had copyright or intellectual property laws for a long time; but as we have seen, these come into conflict with new technologies and practices that alter the terms under which information can be commodified or "owned" by one group apart from another. This scenario, Lyotard admits, is not original or without precedent, but it does allow us to understand the effects of the transformation of knowledge on public power and civil institutions, and it raises afresh the central problem of *legitimation*. Who decides what is "true" or what is to be regarded as "scientific," as properly belonging to the discourse of a scientific community? When knowledge and power are regarded as two sides of the same question, the problem of legitimation of knowledge necessarily comes to the fore, and is no longer seen as solely an internal question of evidence or substantiation: "In the computer age, the question of knowledge is now more than ever a question of government" (Lyotard, 1984: 9).

Others have stressed the interdependent relationship between liberal conceptions of reason and liberal politics, between "how knowledge is conceived

and described by liberal philosophers and how liberal political, juridical, social and economic institutions are constituted" (Ryan, 1988: 154). Hence, science has become a reason of state (Nandy, 1988): not only in how it is typically funded (directly through grants for research; indirectly through
subsidies to government-supported industries), but also in how salient problems (and methods) get defined and prioritized in light of available funding.
This process has long been at work in the field of educational research. Thus
views of progress in knowledge are closely linked with opinions about political progress, economic development, and, in many instances, the pursuit of
national self-interest. Science has been subjected to a new rationalization designed to optimize its contribution to system performance.

That science has become a reason of state tied to the politics of national development is not a recent phenomenon: the relation of science to development
was cemented during and immediately after the Second World War, playing a
focal role in the politics of the Cold War. Arguably, indeed, modern science
was *fundamentally* conceived as a reason of state: even Francis Bacon conceived of science as power over both nature and humanity in the service of
the king (Petitjean et al., 1992). Increasingly since World War II, science and
technology have been recognized as playing fundamental and determining
roles in relation to socioeconomic development. A number of factors have re-
inforced and highlighted this recognition: the relation between new forms of
multidisciplinary basic science and emerging generic technologies (e.g., elec-
tronics, information and communications, advanced materials and biotech-
nology); the role of these generic technologies in driving economic development; the consequent need for countries to fund future-oriented programs of
basic mission-oriented or strategic research; and the changed external
"boundary conditions" under which the scientific research system must now
operate given that science has entered a "steady state" (Ziman, 1994) where
demands for public accountability and "value-for-money" necessarily imply
greater selectivity in the allocation of funds and more systematic approaches
to planning.

For Lyotard, then, two important changes have taken place regarding the
essential mechanisms of scientific research: first, "a multiplication in methods of argumentation and a rising complexity in the process of establishing
proof" (1984: 41). Scientific research, he maintains, has already used methods (languages) outside the concept of classical reason. Second, the production of proof has fallen under the control of another "game," that of technology—a "knowledge game" opposed to that of science (which has as its
disinterested goal "truth")—to one based on the principle of optimal performance and efficiency. Lyotard's analysis here borrows from the concept of
"language games" in the later Wittgenstein, demonstrating the way in which

"progress" in knowledge is subordinated to investment in technology (1984: 58). A new historical dynamic is set up between "being right" and research expenditure; where cost-benefit analyses normally seen as irrelevant to the pursuit of truth suddenly begin to steer that process; where we encounter "an equation between wealth, efficiency and truth" (1984: 45); and where science itself becomes a major force of production, a movement in the circulation of capital. Because education is itself seen, increasingly, as a public investment in social and economic development (increasingly under the rubric of "human capital" or "human resource" development), educational research has been especially subject to this "performative" logic of public funding and public control.

And so we see a distinctive quality to poststructuralism's conception of the "aims" of educational research, which are, at one level, to produce knowledge. But what "knowledge" has come to mean and what it means to "produce" legitimate knowledge today are matters that poststructuralism refuses to take for granted or view simply in epistemological terms. It wants to ask new questions about the ways in which the justification or legitimation of knowledge becomes inseparable from the matter of who is investigating it, with what motives, with what funding and support, and answerable to which constituencies or agendas.

This perspective, in turn, raises specific questions for the subject of this book: What kind of "knowledge game" is educational research? What are the rules that constitute it? What are the stakes? Who are the players? What are their motivations and purposes? Lyotard provides us with a method for analyzing the "games" or paradigms that define the major legitimate (i.e., fundable, publishable, marketable) approaches of educational research. His critique raises questions about the patterns of funding, the "ownership" of knowledge, the commodification of research, and its relation to a political and economic system: To what extent are the forms of legitimate educational research directed toward maximizing the overall efficiency of that system?

REFERENCES

Chalmers, Alan. 1990. *Science and Its Fabrication*. Milton Keynes, U.K.: Open University Press.

Dreyfus, Hubert, and Paul Rabinow. 1982. *Michel Foucault: Beyond Structuralism and Hermeneutics*. Brighton, U.K.: Harvester Press.

Foucault, Michel. 1973. *The Order of Things: An Archaeology of the Human Sciences*. New York: Random House, Vintage Books edition.

———. 1979. *The History of Sexuality*. Vol. 1. London: Allen Lane, Penguin.

——. 1980. *Power/Knowledge: Selected Interviews and Other Writings 1972–1977*. Edited by Colin Gordon. London, Harvester.

——. 1991. *Discipline and Punish: The Birth of the Prison*. Translated by Alan Sheridan. Harmondsworth, U.K.: Penguin.

——. [1977] 1992. *The Archaeology of Knowledge*. Translated by A. M. Sheridan Smith. New York: Routledge.

——. 1997. *Michel Foucault: Ethics, Subjectivity, and Truth*. The Essential Works of Michel Foucault 1954–1984. Vol 1. Edited by Paul Rabinow. London: Allen Lane, The Penguin Press.

Fraser, Nancy. 1981. "Foucault on Modern Power: Empirical Insights and Normative Confusions." *Praxis International* 1: 272–87.

Gay, Peter. 1970. *The Enlightenment: An Interpretation*. London: Weidenfeld and Nicholson.

Habermas, Jürgen. 1971. *Knowledge and Human Interests*. Translated by J. Shapiro. Boston: Beacon Press.

Harding, Sandra. 1991. *Whose Science? Whose Knowledge? Thinking from Women's Lives*. Milton Keynes, U.K.: Open University Press.

Heidegger, Martin. 1996. "Letter on Humanism." In *Basic Writings*. Edited by David Farrell Krell. New York: Routledge.

Hume, David. [1888] 1958. *A Treatise of Human Nature*. Oxford: Clarendon Press. Reprinted from the original edition in three volumes and edited, with an analytical index, by L. A. Selby-Bigge.

Kamenka, Eugene. 1978. "The Anatomy of an Idea." In *Human Rights*. Edited by Eugene Kamenka and Alice Erh-Soon Tay. New York: St. Martin's Press.

Kristeller, Paul Oskar. 1988. "Humanism." Edited by Charles B. Schmitt and Quentin Skinner. *The Cambridge History of Renaissance Philosophy*. Cambridge: Cambridge University Press.

Lyotard, Jean-François. 1984. *The Postmodern Condition: A Report on Knowledge*. Translated by G. Bennington and B. Massumi. Minneapolis: University of Minnesota Press.

Mahon, Michael. 1992. *Foucault's Nietzschean Genealogy: Truth, Power and the Subject*. New York: State University of New York Press.

Marx, Karl. 1977. "On the Jewish Question." In *Karl Marx: Selected Writings*. Edited by David McLellan. Oxford: Oxford University Press.

Nandy, Ashis, ed. 1988. *Science, Hegemony and Violence: A Requiem for Modernity*. New Delhi: Oxford University Press.

Nietzsche, Friedrich. 1974. *The Gay Science*. Translated with a commentray by Walter Kaufmann. New York: Vintage Books.

Peters, Michael A. 1996. *Poststructuralism, Politics, and Education*. Westport, Conn., and London: Bergin and Garvey.

——. 1997. "What is Poststructuralism? The French Reception of Nietzsche." *Political Theory Newsletter* 8, 2: 39–55.

Petitjean, Patrick, Catherine Jami, and Ann Marie Moulin, eds. 1992. *Science and Empires*. Dordrecht, Netherlands: Kluwer.

Phillips, D. C., and Nicholas C. Burbules. 2000. *Postpositivism and Educational Research*. Lanham, Md.: Rowman & Littlefield.

Rabinow, Paul. 1997. "Preface and Afterword." In *Michel Foucault: Ethics, Subjectivity, and Truth, The Essential Works of Michel Foucault 1954–1984*. Vol.1. Translated by R. Hurley et al., edited by Paul Rabinow. London: Penguin.

Rouse, Joseph. 1987. *Knowledge and Power: Toward a Political Philosophy of Science*. Ithaca, N.Y.: Cornell University Press.

Ryan, Michael. 1988. "Deconstruction and Social Theory: The Case of Liberalism." Pp. 154–68 in *Displacement: Derrida and After*. Edited by M. Krupnick. Bloomington: Indiana University Press.

Ziman, John. 1994. *Prometheus Bound: Science in a Steady State*. Cambridge: Cambridge University Press.

3

Poststructuralism, Educational Research, and Methodology: Recent Poststructuralist Research in Education

In recent years, poststructuralism has entered into the realm of educational research. Cleo Cherryholmes's *Power and Criticism: Poststructuralist Investigations*, a landmark text in this regard, was an early attempt to rethink educational discourses and discursive practices from a poststructuralist point of view. Cherryholmes begins his argument by distinguishing poststructuralism from its predecessor:

> Poststructuralist thought attacks structuralist assumptions and the arguments built upon them. Deconstruction, which is one form of poststructural criticism, questions whether proposed first principles that purportedly ground structuralist programs and meanings ever transcend our texts and discourse-practices. . . . Another form of poststructural criticism investigates the effects of history and power on what we claim to know and how we organize our discourse-practices. . . . Together these bodies of thought question the liberal faith in rationality, control, and progress that is repeatedly expressed in educational texts and discourse-practices. (1988: 13–14)

Cherryholmes is referring here to Derrida's deconstruction and Foucault's analysis of discourse. In this chapter we examine poststructural approaches to educational research in some detail, but we are reluctant to construe *deconstruction* or *archaeology* as *methods*, though both certainly have significantly influenced choices of method in educational research. Cherryholmes registers his understanding of this point—that we ought not to regard either deconstruction or archaeology as methods in any reductive sense—by referring instead to poststructural forms of *criticism*. This is a useful way of framing the issue because it avoids reducing complex forms of philosophical thought to a handy set of methods or tools. (Indeed, these poststructural approaches would have us question even the reliance on such instrumentalist metaphors). Recall that poststructuralism as an intellectual movement developed as a specific philosophical response to the scientistic pretensions of structuralism.

Other educational theorists and researchers also see the relevance of post-structural theories of discourse and discursive practices to educational research. In the *Review of Research in Education*, for instance, Allan Luke begins his introduction to "critical discourse analysis" by acknowledging the relations between language, discourse, and education in postmodern conditions by making a very Foucauldian point:

> If we take seriously lessons from the sociology of science, it would be unwise to interpret paradigm shifts in educational research in terms of the succession of disciplinary truths, the emergence of more refined and exacting methods, and a continually improving "state of the art." To embrace such a view of research . . . would be to define educational research first and foremost as a positivist and empiricist enterprise. . . . [E]ducational research is mediated by a complex political economy that entails the immediate statements and imperatives of the institutions it serves; the politics of the academies, government funding agencies, and corporations where theory, research and curriculum work is undertaken; and larger political and economic interests that influence what can be said, by whom, and in what terms across and within institutions. (1997: 3)

Luke proceeds to outline broad demographic and social changes that have occurred since the Second World War before describing the much-heralded "linguistic turn" in the social sciences and its attendant effects on educational research through theories of psycholinguistics, sociolinguistics, and the ethnography of communication—and finally, through the emergence of critical discourse analysis based upon the work of Michel Foucault.

Foucault's analysis of discourse, particularly its *constitutive* character within a broader social formation and its role in the power/knowledge positioning of the subject, play a central role in Luke's analysis. Luke writes: "The principal methodological contribution of Foucault's poststructuralism has been to reinforce skepticism toward the transparency of talk, interview data, and recounts as unproblematic sources of information about 'reality' and 'truth,' 'intent' and 'motivation'" (1995: 7). Hence, apart from the influence of Foucault's studies of disciplining institutions and practices (such as classification systems, examination—both in the sense of testing and of panoptic observation—and governmentality) on the ways in which educational institutions and practices are critically understood, Foucault's influence on educational research and method, as in the social sciences more broadly, has been to provide an account of what counts as the analysis of discourse in educational texts of all kinds (policy documents, the media, curriculum statements, lesson transcripts, *and research writings*). This approach also focuses on the question of subjectivity (subjectivity in itself, as well as the subjectivity of various student populations) as it affects our understanding of methodological concepts such as the "voice" of the interviewee, "fly on the wall" conceptions of ethnography, and the nature of general versus particular claims to knowledge, as in case studies. In short, a Foucauldian approach situates the act of educational research and choices of theory and methodology as themselves implicated in the power/knowledge nexus: For example, one can study classification systems in educational institutions—but it is a deeper level of analysis to reflect upon how research typically becomes a classification system itself.

In her account of *narrative research* in education—including (auto)biographies, bildungsroman, life writing, personal narratives, narrative interviews, life histories, oral histories, ethnohistories, ethnobiographies, and so on—Kathleen Casey (1995) provides a Foucauldian explanation for this shift in methodology by drawing attention to the historical conditions of its emergence and formation, specifically the rising narcissism and fragmentation associated with postmodernism's so-called death of the subject, which is often seen as a central aspect of the developing culture of late capitalism. Casey also considers the reconstructive possibilities inherent in developing more historically complex and nuanced concepts of self and agency. She then outlines an emerging problematic in narrative research, moving beyond narcissism and fragmentation to address narrative responses to existential predicaments, political commitments, and other postmodern dilemmas.

Maxine Greene also discusses the influence of recent poststructuralist and postmodernist approaches to knowledge in educational research. She remarks that over the years we have learned a considerable amount concerning human cognition, individual differences, reading and writing capabilities, giftedness, retardation, assessment, and classroom management; but that at the same time there has developed a disenchantment with technical knowledge and approaches. With the demise of foundationalism, the valorization of multiple realities, and the challenge to objectivism, she argues, poststructuralist and postmodernist approaches to knowledge construction have developed among multiculturalists, hermeneuticists, feminists, and those who utilize the tools of literary criticism. Greene comments: "The deconstructionist critique may in time become relevant for educational researchers perturbed about what is 'normal' and 'real' and whether discourse does or does not refer to a 'world'" (1994: 446).

These attempts to discuss poststructuralism and postmodernism in educational research have not always met with approval or even with informed and sympathetic theoretical understanding. Sometimes they have been challenged by critics who have little direct familiarity with the ideas at stake. In *Educational Researcher*, Mark Constas suggests that postmodernism confronts educational research with destabilizing and profound challenges, but he makes no attempt to distinguish poststructuralism from postmodernism, or to identify their different theoretical homes or trajectories; hence, when he talks of postmodernism he is often discussing aspects of poststructuralism. First, Constas complains that postmodernist educational researchers have accorded narrative a privileged epistemological status, even though such a stance is against the spirit of both Lyotard and Foucault. He argues that "the fascination with narrative methodology and the disregard for systematic inquiry have no foundation in postmodernism . . . or poststructuralism" (Constas, 1998: 28). It is not clear to us what this argument is designed to achieve. Certainly, narrative is not a distinctively poststructuralist or postmodernist mode of inquiry; the contemporary focus on narrative, it could be argued, emerges out of many diverse and contradictory sources: Continental hermeneutics (and especially the work of Hans-Georg Gadamer and Paul Ricoeur) and the structuralist critique of thinkers such as Genet and Greimas. But neither of these movements can be described as postmodern. Conflating poststructural and postmodern ideas with each other, and then linking both in turn with qualitative views of methodology, does more to muddy the waters than to clarify them.

Second, Constas writes: "Many writers who work under the banner of postmodernism seem to display either a limited inclination to arrive at conclusions or an inflated sense of what might be possible within the postmodern framework. Neither of these genres of writing is capable of providing useful guidelines for action that lead to the improvement of educational practice" (1998: 28). In this passage Constas reveals an important assumption within his own view of research: that it must reach "conclusions" and "useful guidelines for action." But many researchers of various methodological stripes, *even rigorously scientific ones*, would argue against these standards as the criteria of credible or worthy educational research, and it seems tendentious to apply them selectively only as a critique against poststructuralist and postmodern research. Constas seems to be recycling oft-repeated criticisms that postmodern discourse is unable to provide practical guidance because its anti-foundationalism "devalue[s] ideals such as progressive improvement, liberation, and unified social resistance" (1998: 29). In response, an ironic postmodernist might reply: My work does support conclusions and ideals, such as: Be suspicious of all ideals based on appeals to progressive improvement! Question the power/knowledge constructions of these sorts of appeals to "liberation." Who instigates such appeals, and for what ends? What groups do such appeals include and which do they exclude? Be wary of the political motives underlying general appeals to "resistance." These are practical guidelines that do implicitly reflect ideals, albeit different ones than Constas might recommend.

Finally, Constas ends by recommending that, given the methodological shift to "narrative methodology," we ought to rethink the way we train educational researchers. But a more careful reading of poststructuralist and postmodernist ideas would have provided a different point of conceptual purchase in discussing the notion of the *human* sciences, which since Descartes and Kant have been based upon the primacy of a centered subjectivity where the human subject was seen as the source of all signification and moral action—contrary to a *structuralist* view of the social sciences that, in the works of Lacan and Lévi-Strauss, purports to explain consciousness and its representations of the world in terms of more fundamental psychological and cultural structures that are themselves not representational. This approach would have provided a better account within which to discuss poststructuralist ideas and their relevance to educational research—and it would have raised a fundamental question about what Constas calls "narrative methodology," which emerged out of the human, hermeneutical sciences, and has relatively little affiliation with most postmodern or poststructural theories.

In line with this argument, therefore, the remainder of the chapter deals with other questions of poststructural methodology, focusing particularly on Foucault's approaches to archaeology, genealogy, and governmentality, Derrida's deconstruction, and, finally, Julia Kristeva's and Luce Irigaray's contributions drawing from linguistics, philosophy, and psychoanalysis.

FOUCAULT: ARCHAEOLOGY, GENEALOGY, AND GOVERNMENTALITY

Three domains of genealogy are possible. First, a historical ontology of ourselves in relation to truth through which we constitute ourselves as subjects of knowledge; second, a historical ontology of ourselves in relation to a field of power through which we constitute ourselves as subjects acting on others; third, a historical ontology in relation to ethics through which we constitute ourselves as moral agents.

—Michel Foucault, "On the Genealogy of Ethics:
An Overview of Work in Progress," *The Foucault Reader*, 114

Archaeology

In the previous chapter we introduced Foucault's notion of the human sciences and his conception of "archaeology"; here we briefly summarize some elements of archaeology before concentrating our attention on "genealogy," which played a greater role in Foucault's later writings. In *The Order of Things* and *The Archaeology of Knowledge*, Foucault used structuralist methods (even though he protested that he was not a structuralist) to investigate the so-called human sciences. In particular, what he shared with structuralist methods is the way in which they displace the primacy of "man" or subjectivity, demonstrating how we can dispense with the model of consciousness that has prevailed since the time of Descartes (and the introspectionist account of meaning and intention based upon it). According to this model, the individual subject is the fount of all knowledge, signification, and moral or political action. Foucault in his early work accepted structuralism as that mode of thought or analysis that reveals or uncovers "deep" psychological structures (Lacan) or cultural structures (Lévi-Strauss), which enables an account of human consciousness and its power to represent the world that itself does not depend upon the model of consciousness and the individual knowing subject. In other words, various adaptations of structural linguistics by, in particular, Lacan, Lévi-Strauss, Louis Althusser, Roland Barthes, and Julia Kristeva, in Foucault's view, enabled a movement beyond entrenched humanist categories of consciousness, subjectivity, and representation that comprise what he called the "problematique" of the subject. (A "problematic" used in this sense means a set of problems to be investigated, held together loosely by a network of beliefs, usually containing core metaphysical propositions protected from intellectual scrutiny.) Foucault's acceptance of certain elements of structuralism allowed him, for instance, to make the famous claim at the end of *The Order of Things* about the disappearance or death of "man," echoing Friedrich Nietzsche's statement that "God is dead." In both contexts, a grounding belief in an entity or concept that guarantees stability, consistency, and predictability across human concerns and actions must be abandoned.

In an interview given in the auspicious year 1968, Foucault is recorded as saying:

[Structuralism] calls into question the importance of the human subject, of human consciousness, of human existence. . . . In a positive manner, we can say that structuralism investigates above all an unconscious. It is the unconscious structures of language, of the literary work, and of knowledge that one is trying at this moment to illuminate. In the second place, I think that one can say that what one is essentially looking for are the forms, the system, that is to say that one tries to bring out the logical correlations that can exist among a great number of elements belonging to a language, to an ideology (as in the analyses of Althusser), to a society (as in Lévi-Strauss), or to different fields of knowledge; which is what I myself have studied. One could describe structuralism roughly as the search for logical structures everywhere they occur. (Foucault, 1994: 653)

In *The Archaeology of Knowledge*, Foucault moved toward articulating a theory of discourse where "discourse" is taken to mean a group of statements that form a unity by virtue of their relation to one another, or, we might say, that belong to the same *discursive formation*. Foucault considered four possibilities for what might constitute such a unity: reference to common objects of analysis, types of statement, systems of concepts, and the theoretical orientation. Where there can be identified clear relations between these elements in an ordered and regular system we might identify a particular discursive formation governed by rules that permit transformations. Foucault, then, provided us with rules for the formation of discourses by emphasizing the systematic relations among the elements that comprise a system. Clearly, Foucault owed a tremendous intellectual debt not only to structural linguistics but also to the applications made by his structuralist contemporaries and colleagues, particularly Georges Canguilhem and Gaston Bachelard.

An increasing number of theorists have used Foucault to engage in archeaological analyses or critiques of educational practices or discourses. Much of the early Foucauldian critique in education focused on discourse analysis of various educational practices or texts, the application of Foucault's ideas on "discipline," and the use of "power/knowledge." For instance, Keith Hoskin puts Foucault himself under examination and questions what he means by "power/knowledge." Hoskin concludes that what Foucault was doing all the time was an *educational* analysis. As he suggests,

> Thus an early work, from his so-called "archaeological" period, like *The Order of Things* (1996), is about nothing other than the nature of certain fields of knowledge—general grammar, natural history, and the analysis of wealth—and their general transformation into other fields—philology, biology, and political economy—fields which, far from being logical consequents, were bizarre dislocations of their antecedents. (1990: 29)

Hoskin demonstrates how Foucault bequeaths us a problem in educational history: how a mode of knowing in the seventeenth and eighteenth centuries—characterizing the representational episteme—becomes transformed into another mode during the nineteenth century. How is the old transformed into the new? How did new learning and knowledges recognizable as our modern disciplines emerge? To answer this educational question Hoskin turns to Foucault's *pouvoir/savoir* (power/knowledge).

Broadhead and Howard (2001) are another example of scholars who use a Foucauldian analysis to examine the United Kingdom's Research Assessment Exercise (RAE) to amplify the nature and practice of disciplinary power in the setting of higher education. They argue that the RAE is a clear and obvious example of Foucault's notion of an "integrated system" of control and production, with its routine operation of surveillance and assessment—and its dependence on coercion and consent.

Genealogy

In terms of methodology, Foucault's move from archaeology to genealogy represents a fundamental shift away from synchronic analyses (models of interrelations within a system at a particular point in time), which are characteristic of structuralism, to diachronic modes of analysis (stressing the development and change of such interrelations across historical epochs) more concerned with the temporal dimension of human culture. The central notion in this latter work is Foucault's analytics of power in relation to evolving knowledge systems, or *epistemes*, that links nondiscursive practices at the level of institutions to systems of discourse or bodies of knowledge. This shift in his thinking from synchronic discourse analysis to diachronic and genealogical analyses of the complex relations between discursive and nondiscursive practices reflects the influence of Nietzsche, especially his notions of genealogy and the will to power, the will to knowledge, and the will to truth (see Nietzsche's *The Genealogy of Morals* and the posthumous *The Will to Power*).

In particular, Foucault is indebted to Nietzsche's linkage between power, knowledge, and truth, which enabled him to analyze social institutions and practices and the complex relations between discursive (bodies of knowledge) and nondiscursive (institutional) practices (see Smart, 1995: 56–60 and Schrift, 1995: 33–101). This shift is most clearly evident in *Discipline and Punish*, discussed in the preceding chapter, which investigated the relations between the emergence of various human sciences and the growth of certain disciplinary practices used in the modern period to control human bodies. *Discipline and Punish*, while focused upon the emergence of the modern penal institution, is explicitly concerned with how the objectification, surveillance, and normalization of the individual subject becomes the central concern for a range of human sciences and institutions. His central interest is the modes of objectification and relations of power/knowledge through which human beings are transformed into subjects *of a certain kind*: a criminal, a delinquent, a good (or bad) student, and so on.

These techniques of disciplinary power operate through *hierarchical observation*, *normalizing judgment*, and the *examination*. The first emphasizes the relation between power and visibility, and many of the closed institutions of the classical age are human "observatories" based upon the military model that permits a one-way gaze and facilitates close scrutiny. The paradigm case here is Jeremy Bentham's "panopticon." The second—normalizing judgment—

establishes conformity and docile bodies through punishment administered according to a schedule of rules and micro-penalties. As Foucault argues:

> The workshop, the school, the army were subject to a whole micro-penalty of time (lateness, absences, interruptions of tasks), of activity (inattention, negligence, lack of zeal), of behavior (impoliteness, disobedience), of speech (idle chatter, insolence), of the body ("incorrect" attitudes, irregular gestures, lack of cleanliness), of sexuality (impurity, indecency). (1979: 178)

The examination, combining the two other technologies and working through the documentation and record of the individual case, effects a "normalizing gaze" on the basis of which individuals can be judged as acceptable or deviant. "Discipline," for Foucault, is a type of power, as he argues, "a modality for its exercise, comprising a whole set of instruments, techniques, procedures, levels of application, targets; it is a 'physics' or an 'anatomy' of power, a technology" (1979: 215).

Foucault's related notion of power also comprises three features. These are summarized well by Gary Gutting:

> First, power is productive. It not only expresses the repressive, exclusionary force of a system's constraints but also creates new domains of knowledge and practice. Second, power is not located in any single control-center; it is dispersed throughout the social system in innumerable local seats of power. These seats interact with one another but do not form a unified system. Third, although it is intimately related to systems of knowledge, power is more than the play of signifiers and signifieds within such systems. It is ultimately the formative action of one body upon another. (1998: 602)

In distinction with traditional views of power, then, power is not just an instrument of repression and control, wielded by some over others; it is a set of relations, some of them productive relations, that may be asymmetrical but that also contain the possibility of resistance and transformation. It is not just a political concept, but an epistemic one: We witness power in ruling institutions and authorities, and even in ways of speaking and thinking.

Drawing these ideas together, "discipline" as a particular mechanism of power, Foucault suggested, emerged during the eighteenth century for the reorganization of a whole set of institutions, including hospitals, clinics, prisons, schools, and factories, and for the mergence of specialized branches of knowledge, including criminology, psychiatry, and pedagogy. The relevance to education and schooling of Foucault's genealogical studies is clearly illustrated in *Discipline and Punish*, including, for example, a long analysis of how the division of the school day into periods with clear schedules and transitions serves not only curricular and organizational purposes, but also teaches submission to a particular order that defines for the subject what can be done, where, and when.

In *The History of Sexuality* (1980) Foucault moved "from a genealogy of the modern individual as object to a genealogy of the modern individual as *subject*" (Schrift, 1995: 49) and speaks of his project as an archaeology of knowledge, a genealogy of normative systems, and an investigation of *subjectivation* or the forms of ethical self-constitution. Thus, in relation to Foucault's investigation of the experience of "sexuality," his analysis, correspondingly, is constituted in terms of: "(1) the formulation of sciences (savoirs) that refer to [sexuality], (2) systems of power that regulate its practice, (3) the forms in which individuals are able, are obliged, to recognize themselves as subjects of this sexuality" (Foucault, 1985: 4).

Foucault's *The History of Sexuality* has proven itself to be remarkably fertile ground for a range of scholars focusing upon relations between "sexuality" and subjectivity (see, for instance, the work of Judith Butler, 1990; 1993). But these ideas and methods of analysis have also yielded fruitful developments and applications in the field of educational research where issues of identity politics loom large and schools have played an important role in the regulation of girls' sexuality. Sue Middleton (1998), for instance, provides a "history of the present" by describing the process of "disciplining the student body" and the changes that took place from the 1920s to the late 1980s.

Educational theorists have been strongly attracted to Foucault's notion of genealogy. James Marshall (1990) talks of Foucault in relation to educational research, and focuses on Foucault as a genealogist, arguing that a genealogical approach would involve shifts in methodology and outcomes. He emphasizes Foucault's *Discipline and Punish* and the way in which Foucault's analysis of power relations requires a very different understanding from traditional liberal or Marxist views. Stephen Ball (1990), in the same collection, picks up on Foucault's notion of technologies to analyze management in education as a "moral technology."

The moral constitution of youth and the ethics of subjectivity is also a theme that runs through Tina Besley's (2002) Foucauldian account of school counseling. Besley analyzes the moral constitution of young people through discourses she calls "psychologizing adolescence" and "sociologizing youth." Her work draws on that of Foucault and Nikolas Rose (1998), whose *Inventing Ourselves: Psychology, Power, and Personhood* provides a Foucauldian analysis of the discursive regime of the self and its animating values of autonomy, identity, individuality, liberty, and choice. He argues that the "psy" disciplines and, in particular, psychology, have played a key role in "inventing ourselves"—inventing new forms of expertise that transform authority into different kinds of therapies and thus change the ethical techniques by which we have come to understand ourselves and act upon ourselves in the *[handwritten annotation]* name of truth (see also Rose 1989; and Peters, 2003a).

See subjectivity section. *[handwritten annotation]*

Governmentality

"Governmentality," a continuation of Foucault's interest in the dynamic between social and political systems of control and practice of self-control, played a larger role in his final works. In his essay "Governmentality" he used the term to mean the art of government and, historically, to signal the emergence of distinctive types of rule that became the basis for modern liberal politics. But this was not just a matter of the state or the political writ large: There was an explosion of interest in the "art of government" in the sixteenth century, motivated by diverse questions such as: the government of oneself (a problematic of personal conduct), the government of souls (a problematic of pastoral doctrine), and the government of children (a problematic of pedagogy). Foucault says that the problematic of government, therefore, can be located at the intersection of two competing tendencies—state centralization and a logic of dispersion. This problematic poses questions about the *how* of government, rather than its legitimation, and seeks "to articulate a kind of rationality which was intrinsic to the art of government without subordinating it to the problematic of the prince and of his relationship to the principality of which he is lord and master" (Foucault, 1991a: 89). It is only in the late sixteenth and early seventeenth centuries, for example, that the art of government crystallizes for the first time around the notion of "reason of state" understood in a positive sense, whereby the state is governed according to rational principles seen as intrinsic to it.

In charting this establishment of the art of government, Foucault thus detailed the introduction of "economy" into political practice, so that "governmentality" is defined in terms of a specific form of government power based upon the "science" of political economy. Over time this shift has transformed the administrative state into one fully governmentalized, and led to the formation of both governmental apparatuses and knowledges (or *savoirs*). In elaborating these themes Foucault concentrated his analytical energies on understanding the multiple forms of modern government, its complexity, and its techniques. He was still interested in the question of how power is exercised in contemporary society, but he came to see it as organized under political mechanisms based in the state while infusing society all the way down to the techniques of "self-government."

In Foucault's terms, governmentality means both governance of self and others. This locates the self as a politically constituted subject and a relevant domain of research. In "Questions of Method," Foucault's inquiry focused on questions such as: Who can govern? What does governing mean? And who is governed? The target of the analysis of governmentality is not

"institutions," "theories," or "ideology," but "'practices"—with the aim of grasping the conditions which make these acceptable at a given moment; the hypotheses being that these types of practice are not just governed by institutions, prescribed by ideologies, guided by pragmatic circumstances . . . but possess up to a point their own specific regularities, logic, strategy, self-evidence and "reason." It is a question of analyzing a regime of practices—practices being understood here as places where what is said and what is done, rules imposed and reasons given, the planned and the taken for granted meet and interconnect. (Foucault, 1991b: 75)

For example, schooling is a site that brings these imperatives of state management and personal formation seamlessly together; relating for example civic or citizenship education, whose content and aims are tied to public behavior and governmental stability, with the formation of character or morality at a personal level through explicit moral education and through the internalized norms of the "hidden curriculum"—learning self-control, taking turns, staying in your seat until given permission to move, and so on. These norms infuse the practices of schooling in all sorts of intentional and invisible ways. Implicitly, Foucault also provides a critique of the contemporary tendency to overvalue the problem of the state as a singularity based upon a certain functionality ("good government"); in modern society the state is active in everything from media content to dietary and fitness standards. Governmentality can be witnessed in the relation between self and itself, interpersonal relations involving some control and guidance, and relations within social institutions and community. The limited conception of power as an institutional and prohibitory phenomenon cannot adequately explain the range of power relations that permeate the body, sexuality, family, kinship, and discourse. The notion of governmentality is, thus, counterposed to statist conceptions of power, which in Foucault's view erroneously dominate modern understandings of social relations. This rejection of narrowly state-centered analyses has become a central feature of the governmentality literature since Foucault.

Foucault's (1982: 221) argument about the strategic reversibility of power relations also requires a theory of governance that presupposes state agency, but that also requires and gains the cooperation of the subject. Governmentality implies the relationship of the self to itself (and to others), referring explicitly to the problem of ethical self-constitution and self-regulation. Thus, it is defined as the set of practices and strategies that individuals in their freedom use in controlling or governing themselves and others. Such an analytics of power bypasses the subject of law, or the strictly legal concept of the subject/citizen, that is demanded by an analysis of power based narrowly upon the institutions of political society. Foucault's point is that if you conceive of the subject only as a subject of law, that is, as one that either has rights or not, then it is difficult to bring out the freedom of the subject and ethical self-constitution in games of freedom. In Foucault's account the relationship of the self to the self is a possible point of resistance to political power, deriving from the Socratic injunction: "Make freedom your foundation, through mastery of yourself." "The task according to Foucault," write the editors of *Foucault and Political Reason*, "was not to denounce the idea of liberty as a fiction, but to analyze the conditions within which the practice of freedom has been possible" (Barry et al., 1996: 8). Foucault provided (1988: 18) an account of these technologies of self and four techniques that human beings employ to interpret, control, and turn themselves into subjects: technologies of domination, technologies of self, technologies of production, and technologies of sign systems.

Marshall (1996, 1998) addresses the question of personal autonomy and freedom in education by emphasizing Foucault's understanding of freedom as an exercise upon or practice of the self. As Marshall explains, the human sciences, including much educational theory that operates as a science, have become manipulative, dominating, and enslaving, turning us into subjects of a certain sort—"docile bodies" classified and constituted as certain kinds of learners (slow, gifted, autonomous, independent, etc.). This analysis reveals dimensions of human freedom and self-constitution that cannot be derived from liberal legal/institutional theories.

Other theorists have made extensive use of Foucault's concept of governmentality. Peters (1996, 2001a, 2001b, 2003b), for instance, has used Foucault's lectures on governmentality to understand the neoliberal paradigm of education policy and the emergence of the entrepreneurial self in education.

DERRIDA AND DECONSTRUCTION

I believe that at a certain level both of experience and of philosophical and scientific discourse, one cannot get along without the notion of the subject. It is a question of knowing where it comes from and how it functions.

—Jacques Derrida, from the discussion following
"Structure, Sign, and Play in the Discourses of the
Human Sciences," p. 271 in *The Structuralist Controversy*

The American reception of deconstruction and the influential formulation of "poststructuralism" in the English-speaking academic world is frequently traced from the essay Derrida delivered, "Structure, Sign, and Play in the Discourse of the Human Sciences," to the International Colloquium on Critical Languages and the Sciences of Man at Johns Hopkins University in October 1966. As we have previously seen (see p. 20), Derrida had forcefully begun to question the ruling megaparadigm of structuralism, and, in his contribution to this conference, he questioned the philosophical assumptions inherent in the idea of "structure," especially that of "centre," which, he argued, froze and limited the play of structure. By this he meant that the question of structure and centre can be understood in terms of a set of metaphors that has its own history, through which we can trace the history of metaphysics—not only "essence," "existence," "substance," and "subject," but also "transcendentality," "consciousness," "God," and "Man." Indeed, all these substitutes for centre or structure conformed to one matrix at least, which Derrida, following Heidegger, suggests is "the determination of being as presence" (Derrida, 1978: 279).

Derrida's aim, then, is to question at a deep cultural level the metaphorical coding of Western metaphysics and the way in which its history has been determined by a succession of what we might call substitution metaphors, where any number of humanist terms have been substituted for centre (the structurality of structure). This stunning insight reveals the extent to which, in the West, the history of metaphysics had not been thought through until Heidegger radically revealed it for what it was: ideological constructions. Taking a leaf from Heidegger, Derrida begins the process of decentering structure and all its substitutions. This decentering calls into question both the transcendental signified and the sovereign subject, and also announces Derrida's sources of inspiration for this radical move in Nietzsche's critique and Heidegger's destruction of metaphysics, and in Freud's critique of self-presence (questioning whether we are transparent to ourselves).

Derrida also signals that two major interpretations are at stake: a Hegelian interpretation symbolized in Lévi-Strauss's work, which dreams of locating a truth or centre that escapes the play of the sign as a basis for a new humanism—that is, a new human certainty, a new humanism found in the absolute truth of structure of language and life; and a Nietzschean inspiration that is suspicious both of "origin" and its equation with "truth" and "centre," and seeks to pass beyond humanism, insofar as it demands a single, unambiguous reading of "man," valid for all time and culture.

The relation of Derridean deconstruction to pedagogy and educational research can be traced as follows: Deconstruction offers an active interpretation of, resistance to, and reevaluation of humanist pedagogy, of forms of pedagogy based on the sovereign subject (which is to say, the predominant forms of pedagogy existing in contemporary institutions, theories, and practices).

Derrida has never disowned the subject or its relevance to philosophical or scientific discourse. He has, however, radically questioned the sovereign subject and the philosophical tradition of consciousness that left its indelible imprint on a variety of postwar humanisms. Inspired by Nietzsche and Heidegger, and befriended by Levinas, Derrida has interrogated the humanist construction of the sovereign subject—its genealogy and its authorial functions—in his attempt to develop a science of writing that both deconstructs and moves beyond "man" as the full presence of consciousness in being.

This focus on the educational centrality of reading and writing is illuminated by Derrida's account of writing as *difference* and the linguistic limit of the subject. *Différance*, as Derrida (1981: 8–9) remarks, is both the common root of all the positional concepts marking our language and the condition for all signification; it refers not only to the "movement that consists in deferring by means of delay, delegation, reprieve, referral, detour, postponement, reserving," but also and finally to "the unfolding of difference," of the onticoontological difference that Heidegger named as the difference between Being and beings. While many of our theoretical frameworks foreground the question of phenomena sharing common traits, strong theories of difference note that it is in *differentiation* that signification and interpretation become possible. The educational impact of such ideas can be seen in trends as disparate as the acceptance of "nonstandard" spellings in early writing instruction, the rejection of required "canons" in many humanities departments in the university, the elevation of readerly prerogatives to freely interpret texts without regard to "authorial intention" as a constraint, and the emergence of strong multiculturalisms that reject melting-pot analogies and urge learners to "celebrate differences."

There have been a number of attempts to apply these ideas to pedagogy. Gregory Ulmer (1985) has outlined a post-Derrida program, especially in the areas of media and cultural studies, that he calls "applied grammatology," where students are encouraged to experience theory directly in performance. His website (www.ucet.ufl.edu/~gulmer) supports the University Lab for Media Electronic Research, including a listserv for "electracy," a form of Internet collaboration he calls "cyberpidgin," "institutional invention," and "electronic learning forum." In a less experimental and, perhaps, more traditionally academic way, Vincent Leitch (1996) also has attempted to apply Derrida's ideas directly to pedagogy, (see especially his chapters "Teaching Deconstructively" and "Postmodernism, Pedagogy, and Cultural Criticism").

Derrida's account of writing also involves the deconstruction of the authorial-authoritarian subject. This is Schrift's way of describing it: "Derrida develops his deconstructive critique of the subject as a privileged center of discourse in the context of his project of delegitimizing authority, whether that authority emerges in the form of the author's domination of the text, or the tradition's reading of the history of philosophy" (1995: 24–25). Derrida's deconstructive critique of authority—both the authority of the text and of the history of philosophy—has an obvious relevance to pedagogy as a critique of the authority of educational institutions and those that assume positions of authority in its name.

In one sense we can understand Derrida's *différance* as a deferral and postponement that entails a decentering of the subject that becomes obvious in pedagogy through the effects of new information and communications technologies. These technologies disassemble and rearrange the old technologies of reading and writing (and the forms of subjectivity associated with them). In particular, they collapse traditional spaces, overturning the classroom as a space of enclosure—the pedagogical machine devoted to reading and writing—to open up new spaces no longer disciplined by the teacher. In the move from enclosed to open spaces, from closed to open systems, the teacher's authority becomes decentered, especially when the "information level" is higher outside the classroom than it is inside, and access to new media is often immediate, unsupervised, and continuous. Yet this does not necessarily mean new freedoms; it may also represent new dangers.

Let us examine more closely Derrida's notion of *deconstruction*. Typically in a deconstructive reading, the text in question is shown to harbor contradictory logics that are often ignored—or concealed from view—through other more orthodox accounts. Very often this internal tension is a matter of locating certain clearly marked binary oppositions (as for instance between nature and culture, speech and writing, concept and metaphor, or philosophy and literature) and showing that their order of priority is by no means as stable or secure as the text seeks to maintain. That is to say, there is a counterlogic at work within the text whereby those distinctions can be shown to break down, or to generate a reading markedly at odds with the author's overt intent (Norris, 1998: 836). Deconstruction also works to disturb the logic that ranks terms in an often implicit hierarchy of values established by the text (not just dichotomizing nature versus culture, but making an implicit valuation of one over the other). One term is given a positive value *at the expense of* the second term. This is clearly the case with Rousseau, as Derrida demonstrates, when he points to the way Rousseau privileges nature over culture as the determinant of a proper education.

As Norris (1998: 837) explains clearly, this deconstructive move is quite different from the analytic tradition in philosophy and also must not be seen simply as a form of literary criticism. Derrida's approach is philosophical: first, by regarding philosophy as a series of texts rather than problems to be worked through; second, by examining problematical passages in certain texts, demonstrating that they are structurally at odds with the logic governing the overall argument. (For example, a celebration of clear, literal exposition in philosophical writing, which itself rests upon a number of expressed metaphors and figurative turns of phrase.) Yet this close textual reading, as Norris argues, ought not to be confused with mere exegesis or the practice of literary criticism (even though it does lend itself to applications as forms of literary analysis), for Derrida is inquiring into

> the conditions of possibility for raising such questions about meaning, context, authorial intention and so forth, questions that clearly point beyond the sphere of localized interpretative insight or thematic commentary. . . . What chiefly engages Derrida's interest is that pervasive "logic of supplementarity" whereby the second (supposedly inferior or derivative) term in each pair turns out to be always already presupposed in any definition of the first (supposedly original and self-sufficient) term. (Norris, 1998: 837)

We see an important parallel here with an idea from Foucault: It is often by studying the "deviants" defined as such by a particular society that we reveal the characteristics and complexities of the "normal"—which are rarely recognized or justified as anything other than natural. By studying how society classifies (or castigates) homosexuals, for example, we learn something about its concerns and anxieties about heterosexuality; by studying who gets counted as "black," we learn how "whiteness" is a color too—and not just an absence of color. (One of our colleagues likes to ask why only one aisle of the grocery store is labeled "ethnic food"—when clearly all food is ethnic, to someone.)

Seen in this light, Derrida's deconstruction has significant potential for educational research. Deconstruction clearly impinges not only directly upon conceptions of "reading" and "writing" and the ways these pedagogical processes have been theoretically represented in the Western tradition; it also provides strong and useful analytical procedures for analyzing texts of all kinds, cultures, institutions, traditions, philosophies, and subjects. Indeed Derrida, of all the major poststructuralist thinkers, has had the most to say about educational practices and policies. He has a long history of engagement with pedagogical and educational issues and institutions, including the group he helped establish in 1975 called the "Research Group for Teaching of Philosophy" (*GREPH: Groupe de Recherches sur l'Enseignement Philosophique*) and the "International College of Philosophy" he helped found with a group of colleagues in 1983. Derrida, in a series of essays, interviews, and talks over the course of his career, has pursued questions concerning philosophical research, the teaching of philosophy, and the relation between philosophy and institutions, particularly the university (see, e.g., Derrida, 2002). His work on these themes is becoming more widely known in education: Denise Egéa-Keuhne (1995, 2001) and Peter Trifonas (2001, 2002, 2003a) have been leading scholars in the field of education addressing Derridean themes of academic responsibility, educational rights, and the voice, idiom, ethics, and teaching of the other.

Derrida and deconstruction have been subjected to intense criticism—often unfairly by people who have not carefully read his work. In particular, deconstruction has been misunderstood as a "method" that can be applied following a number of steps or a set of rules. Derrida has been very careful to not provide such reductionist or formulaic definitions of deconstruction in order to prevent slavish imitation. At a roundtable conversation at Villanova University to celebrate the inauguration of the new doctoral program in philosophy, Derrida (1994b: 5) was careful from the outset to insist that deconstruction has never opposed institutions as such, and to emphasize affirmative deconstruction as that which "repeats" the institution yet in a transformative and critical way that opens it to its own future. Along with this "affirmation" comes a certain kind of responsibility not limited simply to the reproductive moment, but moving in the direction of newness, novelty, and originality. John Caputo, talking of deconstruction in a nutshell, elaborates this point:

> The very meaning and mission of deconstruction is to show that things—texts, institutions, traditions, societies, beliefs, and practices . . .—do not have definable meanings and determinable missions, that they are always more than any mission would impose, that they exceed boundaries they currently occupy. . . . A "meaning" or a "mission" is a way to contain and compact things, like a nutshell, gathering them into a unity, whereas deconstruction bends all its efforts to stretch beyond those boundaries, to transgress these confines, to interrupt and disjoin all such gathering. (1998: 31–32)

Caputo then moves on to discuss under the notion of the "anxieties of indignation" the common misunderstandings of Derrida. This following passage is worthy of note because it helps clear away misinformation about deconstruction that many who have not read Derrida are inclined to repeat. Caputo writes:

> The most fundamental misunderstanding to beset Derrida is the mistaken impression that is given of a kind of anarchistic relativism in which "anything goes." On this view, texts mean anything the reader wants them to mean; traditions are just monsters to be slain or escaped from; the great masters of the Western tradition are dead white male tyrants whose power must be broken and whose names defamed; institutions are just power-plays oppressing everyone; and language is a prison, just a game of signifiers signifying nothing, a play of difference without reference to the real world. (1998: 37–38)

By contrast, Caputo claims, Derrida's deconstruction actually *affirms* what is to come. It deconstructs the present and "the values of presence" in support of democracy, justice, and, in certain contexts, even a pedagogy yet to come. What might a decentered and radically democratic pedagogy look like? What possibilities are there with new media and communications technologies for creating democratic pedagogies rather than simply better customized or tailored learning strategies to accommodate learning consumers? Does the shift from "teaching" and "education" in a formal, structured, and institutional sense to unstructured, open, and distance systems, where the focus falls increasingly on the learner, open up the possibilities for radically new pedagogies that can recognize and better accommodate difference? These are some of the e-learning issues that Derrida encourages us to imagine.

KRISTEVA AND IRIGARAY: WOMEN AS OTHER

One complex strand of poststructuralist thinking involves the work of women writers, often referred to as poststructuralist feminists and typically thought to include Julia Kristeva, Luce Irigaray, and Hélène Cixous. Sometimes the work of Anne Schneider is also mentioned. The genealogy of "French poststructuralist feminism" is often seen to be "double": to be traced, on the one hand, through their engagement with the philosophical and psychoanalytical texts that constitute the entire Western tradition (but focusing upon Nietzsche and Lacan, respectively) and on the other hand through the texts that comprise French feminism, beginning with or giving special precedence to the work of Simone de Beauvoir. We reject this interpretation and the attempt to homogenize the "French poststructuralist feminist": the women writers to whom we refer are very different from one another; they work out of different traditions, and draw upon different sources of inspiration for their work. In this sense it is difficult to characterize a "movement" here in any strict sense; yet, taken together, their work does represent an important aspect of French poststructuralism—some would argue its cutting edge. Any account of the relation of poststructuralism to educational research, therefore, requires consideration of the work of these thinkers that, through its focus on questions of women's identity and alterity, demonstrates both its relevance and significance to contexts of education. It is, of course, impossible here to do justice to the entire scope, complexity, diversity, and theoretical subtleties of this body of work, so we have focused upon aspects of the work of Julia Kristeva and Luce Irigaray in an introductory way to make the case for the particular significance of their work to educational research. We will approach their work as offering examples of the ways in which these thinkers theorize questions of alterity and identity in relation to women.

If there is one "truth" or fundamental principle that poststructuralist thought has contested, it is the notion of self-consciousness and the self-conscious subject who is said to be self-transparent, or identifies itself with itself through an act of self-knowledge. Even Hegel criticized the abstract nature of Descartes' ego. Hegel sought to explain the identity of the self as mediated by the other (as in his famous analysis of master and slave, who are opposed to each other in their asymmetrical power, but who each define and realize themselves only in relation to the other). This Hegelian dialectic of self and other—seen by Cixous to be based on an account of property—is, however, based upon a concept of the self-mediating whole that many poststructuralists reject. Drawing instead upon the work of Nietzsche and Freud, who analyzed consciousness as a secondary process governed by the unconscious or the will, a number of important French thinkers (including Jacques Lacan and Georges Bataille) who followed Alexandre Kojève's interpretation of Hegel's dialectic as a logic of human *desire* sought to define desire in terms of the other. Lacan, for instance—the French psychoanalyst who gave a "structuralist" reading of Freud—defines desire in this way (see Penves, 1998). This centrality of the other as a challenge to and reflection upon one's self-awareness is a theme recurring in poststructuralist thought; in educational contexts, it suggests that a primary reason for studying other cultures and traditions is not just out of curiosity, empathy, or tolerance for them, but also as a window into a better and more critical understanding of ourselves.

It is in this general intellectual context that we might first locate the writing of Kristeva and Irigaray. Kristeva combines psychoanalytic thought with linguistics to analyze language as a signifying system operating in terms of semiotic and symbolic dimensions that integrate both the "voice," the bodily, and kinetic, on the one hand, with the social and the cultural on the other, thus emphasizing the complex interactions between the material world and representation. This semiotic-symbolic analysis of language enables her to provide highly dynamic, process-oriented, and complex readings of literary, philosophical, and historical texts as well as cultural phenomena. The best introduction to Kristeva's approach to linguistics is *The Revolution in Poetic Language* ([1974] 1984) and the text that marks her decisive turn to psychoanalysis, *Powers of Horror: An Essay on Abjection* (1982).

In the former text, Kristeva elaborates the *semiotic* modality of language by reference to concepts from Freudian depth psychology: drives, the unconscious, and the pre-Oedipal. The *symbolic*, by contrast, is understood by reference to the function of representation and language as a signifying system. The semiotic drives create the *chora*, a notion that Kristeva retrieves from

Plato, to stand as the maternal and generative place, both formless and undeterminable, that nevertheless converts the semiotic into the symbolic, thus subjecting the instinctual and the bodily to the ordering of culture. In this latter text, Kristeva famously provides a Lacanian analysis of alterity in terms of the other, the *alter ego*, and the "other" as an object of desire, focusing upon the "abject" or utterly undesirable—that which escapes the dialectics of desire (once again, consider Foucault's point about the "deviant" and the "normal"). The abject is that which, according to Kristeva, the self perceives as both preceding, and threatening to engulf, the self and is therefore violently expelled. Many forms of religious discourse that make central the categories of purification and personal defilement can be understood in terms of abjection, Kristeva argues (see Oliver, 1993; Chanter, 1998a). These issues of depth psychology theorized by Kristeva provide a new lens for understanding education and schooling at the levels of the unconscious and the symbolic—not merely the schooling of the educational self and its others but also the way in which transference and countertransference enter into the pedagogical relation.

Luce Irigaray is also interested in linguistics, philosophy, and psychoanalysis. Indeed, Irigaray holds doctorates in both linguistics and philosophy, and practiced as a psychoanalyst. Her early works, *Speculum of the Other Woman* ([1974] 1985b) and *This Sex Which Is Not One* ([1977] 1985a) constitute a critique of the ways in which the masculine subject, dominant in the Western philosophical tradition, has constructed the world and interpreted it according to its singular perspective. In this critique Irigaray demonstrates how pervasive this "phallocentric" view is in the Western philosophical tradition by providing close textual encounters with Plato, Plotinus, Descartes, Hegel, and Freud; through this reexamination she begins to excavate the layers of the problem of women as the Other within Western culture. The essay "When Our Lips Speak Together" (in *This Sex Which Is Not One*), which plays on and against Lacan's notion of the "phallus," is an attempt to create a contrasting female imaginary in order to counter the dominant masculine one. This project represents the first stage of her work, which she divides into three phases. As Tina Chanter observes:

> The second stage, in which one might include *Sexes and Genealogies* [1993c], was one in which she [Irigaray] defined "a second subject," that of a "feminine subjectivity." The third phase, represented by *Je, tu, nous* [1990] [*Je, Tu, Nous: Toward a Culture of Difference*, 1993b], is one in which she constructs "an intersubjectivity respecting sexual difference." (1998b: 1)

In the second phase, Irigaray makes greater use of psychoanalysis to study feminine sexuality in terms of myth and religion, and directly engages with

Nietzsche (*The Marine Lover of Friedrich Nietzsche*, 1991) and a range of other philosophers both ancient and contemporary (especially in *An Ethics of Sexual Difference*, 1993a). In the third phase, we might argue that Irigaray focuses more directly upon the notion of sexual difference, attempting to build an ethics that involves a genuine respect for difference between men and women. This shift to an "intersubjectivity of sexual difference" and an ethics of sexual difference is seen, perhaps, most clearly in *I Love To You* (1996).

The thought of Kristeva and Irigaray, in the context of education and educational research, foregrounds questions of gender, of female subjectivity, of sexual difference, of desire, and of feminine identity. Both thinkers offer a range of sophisticated modes of analysis, drawing upon philosophy, linguistics, and psychoanalysis. Together, though differently, they deconstruct the "maleness" (phallocentrism) of Western culture and thought, providing new ways of constructing a feminine imaginary, culture, way of writing, and, very positively, an ethics of difference. Educationalists, especially feminist educational thinkers and researchers, have only recently begun the task of "translating" and developing these concerns into a form that has its uses in educational theory and practice.

Lucy Holmes, for instance, remarks that educational sociology has been criticized for being theoretically underdeveloped, particularly in the areas of identity-formation and socialization. She recalls how Kristeva draws our attention to Barthes' understanding of literature as a textual and literary practice, and she indicates how this understanding, when perceived by Kristeva in the 1960s, provided a way of connecting the individual with structures. Holmes argues: "For Kristeva the missing link is literary or textual production as practical knowledge of how the production of meaning plays a part in the constitution of a subject and in ideological traditions" (1998: 86).

Kristeva has consistently denied she is a feminist, whereas Luce Irigaray happily accepts this label. Betsan Martin (1998) provides an analysis of her work that leads us to question the universal rational male subject and its influence on education. She makes the point, now well-taken, that women are represented as the object of male desire in Western culture and that the training ground for this kind of socializing starts early in school. In particular, Martin traces an ethics of sexual difference in Irigaray's work in a way designed to explore women's subjectivity and women becoming subjects.

Indeed, the question of sexual difference and of women's subjectivity has led to a host of new studies, often directly motivated by poststructuralist feminism, in related areas of postcoloniality, race and representation, understanding emotion, black femininities and masculinities, and queer pedagogies—all as a means for rethinking education for social change (see, e.g., Trifonas, 2003b).

REFERENCES

Ball, Stephen. 1990. "Management as Moral Technology." In *Foucault and Education*. Edited by S. Ball. London: Routledge.

Barry, A. T. Osborne, and N. Rose, eds. 1996. *Foucault and Political Reason: Liberalism, Neo-liberalism, and Rationalities of Government*. London: U.C.L. Press.

Besley, Tina. 2002. *Counseling Youth: Foucault, Power, and the Ethics of Subjectivity*. Westport, Conn.: Praeger.

Broadhead, L. A., and S. Howard. 2001. "'The Art of Punishing': The Research Assessment Exercise and the Ritualisation of Power in Education." *Educational Policy Analysis* 6, 8. Available at http://olam.ed.asu.edu/epaa/v6n8.html (accessed September 1, 2003).

Burchell, G. 1996. "Liberal Government and Techniques of the Self." Pp. 19–36 in *Foucault and Political Reason*. Edited by Andrew Barry, Thomas Osborne, and Nikolas Rose. London: U.C.L. Press.

Butler, Judith. 1990. *Gender Trouble: Feminism and the Subversion of Identity*. New York: Routledge.

——. 1993. *Bodies That Matter: On the Discursive Limits of "Sex."* New York: Routledge.

Caputo, John, ed. 1998. *Deconstruction in a Nutshell: A Conversation with Jacques Derrida*. New York: Fordham University Press.

Casey, Katherine. 1995. "The New Narrative Research in Education." *Review of Research in Education* 21: 211–53.

Chanter, Tina. 1998a. "Kristeva, Julia (1941–)." Pp. 305–8 in *Routledge Encyclopedia of Philosophy*. Edited by E. Craig. New York: Routledge.

——. 1998b. "Irigaray, Luce (1930–)." Pp. 1–4 in *Routledge Encyclopedia of Philosophy*. Edited by E. Craig. New York: Routledge.

Cherryholmes, Cleo. 1988. *Power and Criticism: Poststructuralist Investigations*. New York: Teachers College Press.

Constas, Mark. 1998. "The Changing Nature of Educational Research and a Critique of Postmodernism." *Educational Researcher* 27, 2: 26–33.

Davidson, Arnold. 1997. "Structures and Strategies of Discourse: Remarks towards a History of Foucault's Philosophy of Language." In *Foucault and His Interlocutors*. Edited and introduced by Arnold I. Davidson. Chicago and London: Chicago University Press.

Derrida, Jacques. 1970. "Structure, Sign, and Play in the Discourses of the Human Sciences." P. 271 in *The Structuralist Controversy*. Edited by Richard Macksey and Eugenio Donato, translated by Richard Macksey. Baltimore, Md.: Johns Hopkins University Press, 1970.

——. 1976. *Of Grammatology*. Translated by G. C. Spivak. Baltimore and London: The Johns Hopkins University Press.

——. 1978. "Structure, Sign, and Play in the Discourses of the Human Sciences." Pp. 278–93. In *Writing and Difference*. Translated by A. Bass. Chicago: University of Chicago Press.

——. 1981. *Positions*. Translated by A. Bass. Chicago: University of Chicago Press.

——. 1982. "The Ends of Man." Pp. 109–36 in *Margins of Philosophy*. Translated by A. Bass. Chicago: University of Chicago Press.

——. 1983. "The Time of the Thesis: Punctuations." Pp. 34–50 in *Philosophy in France Today*. Edited by Alan Montefiore. Cambridge: Cambridge University Press.

——. 1985. "Otobiographies: The Teaching of Nietzsche and the Politics of the Proper Name." Edited by Avital Ronell. Pp. 1–38 in *The Ear of the Other: Otobiography, Transference, Translation*. English edition edited by Christie V. McDonald. Translated by Peggy Kamuf. New York: Schocken Books.

——. 1994a. "Nietzsche and the Machine: An Interview with Jacques Derrida by Richard Beardsworth." *Journal of Nietzsche Studies* 7: 7–66.

——. 1994b. "Roundtable Discussion with Jacques Derrida." Transcribed by J. Christian Guerrero. Villanova University, October 3, 1994. Available at www.hydra.umn.edu/derrida/vill1.html (accessed September 1, 2003).

——. 2002. *Who's Afraid of Philosophy?* Right to Philosophy I. Translated by Jan Plug. Stanford: Stanford University Press.

Egéa-Keuhne, Denise. 1995. "Deconstruction Revisited and Derrida's Call for Responsibility." *Educational Theory* 45, 3: 293–309.

——. 2001. "Derrida's Ethics of Affirmation: The Challenge of Educational Rights and Responsibility." In *Derrida and Education*. Edited by Gert J. J. Biesta and Denise Egéa-Kuehne. London and New York: Routledge.

Foucault, Michel. 1979. *Discipline and Punish: The Birth of the Prison*. Translated by Alan Sheridan. New York: Vintage Books.

——. 1980. *The History of Sexuality*. Vol. 1. New York: Vintage Books.

——. 1982. "Afterword: The Subject and Power." In *Michel Foucault: Beyond Structuralism and Hermeneutics*. H. Dreyfus and P. Rabinow. Chicago: The Harvester Press.

——. 1984. "On the Genealogy of Ethics: An Overview of Work in Progress." In *The Foucault Reader*. Edited by Paul Rabinow. New York: Pantheon Books.

——. 1985. *The Use of Pleasure*. Translated by Robert Hurley. New York: Random House.

——. 1988. "Technologies of the Self." Pp. 16–49 in *Technologies of the Self: A Seminar with Michel Foucault*. Edited by Martin, Luther H., Huck Gutman, and Patrick H. Hutton. London, U.K.: Tavistock.

——. 1991a. "Governmentality." Pp. 87–104 in *The Foucault Effect: Studies in Governmentality*. Edited by G. Burchell, C. Gordon, P. Miller. Hemel Hempstead, U.K.: Harvester Wheatsheaf Press.

——. 1991b. "Questions of Method" Pp. 87–104 in *The Foucault Effect: Studies in Governmentality*. Edited by G. Burchell, C. Gordon, and P. Miller. Hemel Hempstead, U.K.: Harvester Wheatsheaf Press.

——. 1994. "Interview with Michel Foucault." (1968). *Dits et écrits, 1954–1988*. Vol 1. Daniel Defert and François Ewald with Jacques Lagrange. 4 vols. Paris: Gallimard.

Greene, Maxine. 1994. "Epistemology and Educational Research—The Influence of Recent Approaches to Knowledge." *Review of Research in Education* 20: 423–64.

Gutting, Gary. 1998. "Post-Structralism in the Social Sciences." Pp. 600–604 in *Routledge Encyclopedia of Philosophy*. Edited by E. Craig. New York: Routledge.

Holmes, Lucy. 1998. "Julia Kristeva: Intertextuality and Education." In *Naming the Multiple: Poststructuralism and Education*. Edited by Michael A. Peters. Westport, Conn., and London: Bergin and Garvey.

Hoskin, Keith. 1990. "Foucault under Examination: The Crypto-Educationalist Unmasked." In *Foucault and Education*. Edited by Stephen Ball. London: Routledge.

Irigaray, Luce. [1977] 1985a. *This Sex Which Is Not One*. Translated by C. Porter with C. Burke. Ithaca, N.Y.: Cornell University Press.

———. [1974] 1985b. *Speculum of the Other Woman*. Translated by G. C. Gill. Ithaca, N.Y.: Cornell University Press.

———. 1991. *The Marine Lover of Friedrich Nietzsche*. Translated by G. C. Gill. New York: Columbia University Press.

———. 1993a. *An Ethics of Sexual Difference*. Translated by C. Burke and G. C. Gill. Ithaca, N.Y.: Columbia University Press.

———. 1993b. *Je, Tu, Nous: Toward a Culture of Difference*. Translated by A. Martin. New York: Routledge.

———. 1993c. *Sexes and Genealogies*. Translated by G. C. Gill. New York: Columbia University Press.

———. 1996. *I Love To You*. Translated by A. Martin. New York: Routledge.

Kristeva, Julia. 1982. *Powers of Horror: An Essay on Abjection*. Translated by L. S. Roudiez. New York: Columbia University Press.

———. [1974] 1984. *The Revolution in Poetic Language*. New York: Columbia University Press.

Leitch, Vincent. 1996. *Postmodernism—Local Effects, Global Flows*. New York: State University of New York Press.

Luke, Allan. 1995. "Text and Discourse in Education: An Introduction to Critical Discourse Analysis." *Review of Research in Education* 21: 3–48.

Lyotard, Jean-François. [1979] 1984. *The Postmodern Condition: A Report on Knowledge*. Translated by Geoff Bennington and Brian Massumi with a foreword by Fredric Jameson. Minneapolis: University of Minnesota Press.

Macksey, Richard, and Eugenio Donato, eds. 1990. *The Structuralist Controversy*. Translated by Richard Macksey. Baltimore, Md.: Johns Hopkins University Press.

Marshall, James D. 1990. *Foucault and Educational Research*. In *Foucault and Education*. Edited by Stephen Ball. London: Routledge.

———. 1996. *Michel Foucault: Personal Autonomy and Education*. London: Kluwer Academic.

———. 1998. "Michel Foucault: Philosophy, Education, and Freedom as an Exercise upon the Self." In *Naming the Multiple: Poststructuralism and Education*. Edited by Michael A. Peters. Westport, Conn., and London: Bergin and Garvey.

Martin, Betsan. 1998. "Luce Irigaray: One Subject Is Not Enough—Irigaray and Levinas Face-to-Face with Education." In *Naming the Multiple: Poststructuralism and Education*. Edited by Michael A. Peters. Westport, Conn., and London: Bergin and Garvey.

Middleton, Sue. 1998. *Disciplining Sexuality: Foucault, Life Histories, and Education*. New York, London: Teachers College, Columbia University.

Norris, Christopher. 1998. "Deconstruction." Pp. 836–39 in *Routledge Encyclopedia of Philosophy*. Edited by E. Craig. New York: Routledge.

Oliver, K., ed. 1993. *Ethics, Politics, and Difference in Julia Kristeva's Writing*. New York: Routledge.

Penves, Peter. 1998. "Alterity and Identity, Postmodern Theories of." Pp. 187–92 in *Routledge Encyclopedia of Philosophy*. Edited by E. Craig. New York: Routledge.

Peters, Michael A. 1996. "Foucault, Discourse, and Education: Neoliberal Governmentality." In *Poststructuralism, Politics, and Education*. Westport, Conn., and London: Bergin and Garvey.

——. 2001a. "Foucault and Governmentality: Understanding the Neoliberal Paradigm of Education Policy." *The School Field* 12, 5–6: 61–72.

——. 2001b. "Education, Enterprise Culture, and the Entrepreneurial Self: A Foucauldian Perspective." *Journal of Educational Enquiry* 2, 1 (May). Available at www.literacy.unisa.edu.au/jee/Papers/JEEVol2No2/200144.pdf (accessed September 10, 2003).

——. 2003a. "Truth-Telling as an Educational Practice of the Self: Foucault, *Parrhesia* and the Ethics of Subjectivity," *Oxford Review of Education* 29, 2: 207–23.

——. 2003b. "The New Prudentialism in Education: Actuarial Rationality and the Entrepreneurial Self." Paper presented at Round Table on "Education and Risk" at the World Congress of Philosophy. Istanbul, August.

Popkewitz, Thomas. 1997. "A Changing Terrain of Knowledge and Power: A Social Epistemology of Educational Research." *Educational Researcher* 26, 9 (December): 18–29.

Popkewitz, Thomas, and Marie Brennan. 1998. *Foucault's Challenge: Discourse, Knowledge, and Power in Education*. New York: Teachers College Press.

Rose, Nikolas. 1989. *Governing the Soul: The Shaping of the Private Self*. New York: Routledge.

——. 1998. *Inventing Ourselves: Psychology, Power, and Personhood*. Cambridge U.K.: Cambridge University Press.

Schrift, Alan. 1995. *Nietzsche's French Legacy: A Genealogy of Poststructuralism*. New York: Routledge.

Smart, Barry. [1995] 2002. *Michel Foucault*. New York: Routledge.

Trifonas, Peter. 2000. *The Ethics of Writing: Deconstruction and Pedagogy*. Lanham, Md.: Rowman & Littlefield.

——. 2001. "Teaching the Other II: Ethics, Writing, Community." Pp. 98–118 in *Derrida and Education*. Edited by Gert J. J. Biesta and Denise Egéa-Kuehne. London and New York: Routledge.

——. 2002. *Ethics, Institutions, and the Right to Philosophy* (with Jacques Derrida). Lanham, Md.: Rowman & Littlefield.

——, ed. 2003a. *Derrida*. Special Issue. *Educational Philosophy and Theory* 35, 3.

——, ed. 2003b. *Pedagogies of Difference: Rethinking Education for Social Change*. London and New York: RoutledgeFalmer.

Ulmer, Gregory. 1985. *Applied Grammatology: Post(e)-pedagogy from Jacques Derrida to Joseph Beuys*. Baltimore: Johns Hopkins University Press.

4

New Practices of Reading and Three Exemplars

INTRODUCTION: NEW PRACTICES OF READING

At its simplest, poststructuralism can be viewed as introducing a new freedom of thought, action, and interpretation after the "death of God" declared by Nietzsche and the consequent demise of absolute truth, foundations, and a final horizon of interpretation. With a loss of God and of all possible God-substitutes, a new interpretive space developed that emphasised a greater fragility of the self—its finitude, corporeality, and freedom. This freedom, no longer guaranteed or based on foundational morality, released the creative, unconscious, and instinctual energies that came to be expressed in a succession of European avant-gardes. It also saw the fusion of the twentieth-century linguistic turn exemplified in the birth of structuralist linguistics and semiology with phenomenological approaches that tended to highlight the body and its perceptual field. In this context, poststructuralist thought—inheriting methods of structural, cultural, and historical analysis and imbued with a new sense of innovation and experimentalism, developed original and powerful critical practices of reading and writing—new ways of reading, writing, and analyzing texts, institutions, history, culture, and the self.

The development of new reading practices is historically grounded in the flourishing of formalist and futurist poetics, and structuralist methods especially in linguistics. Its first impulse can be seen in pre-revolutionary Russia with the setting up of linguistic circles in Moscow and St. Petersburg by the luminary Roman Jakobson, and later in Prague and Geneva and other European capitals. Jakobson later brought his new structuralist methods to New York and Paris in the early forties, strongly influencing Claude Lévi-Strauss who modeled his anthropology on structuralist methodology. Such developments promised not only

81

a rigorous method but also a renewed scientificity, although scientific structuralism, represented particularly in the work of Lévi-Strauss and Jacques Lacan, was contemporaneous with both a *semiological* structuralism in the work of Roland Barthes, Gerard Genette, and Tzvetan Todorov, and a *historicized* or *epistemic* structuralism, represented by Althusser, Foucault, Derrida, and members of the *Annales* group (see Dosse, 1997).

In terms of these developments, particularly once the scientific strand had given way to subtler and more nuanced versions, new *readings* (and writings) of classic thinkers in the Western canon (Marx, Freud, Nietzsche)—readings in the plural—became possible and expected. In this regard Terell Carver writes: "There have always been multiple Marxes, and each one is a product of a reading strategy. A reading strategy involves a choice of texts in a biographical frame, philosophical presuppositions about language and meaning, and political purpose—whether acknowledged or not" (1998: 234). He suggests that the "linguistic turn" of Western intellectual history in the twentieth century led to the priority of "the textual surface," a shift away from "the reality that language purportedly described, and toward the subjects (writers and audiences) and objects (meaningful activities or 'discursive practices') that language was said to construct or constitute" (1998: 7). Carver, in the main, is correct in his assertion, although we might further supplement his analysis by saying that the linguistic turn represents a shift in thinking that takes place simultaneously across the disciplines in linguistics, philosophy, the visual arts, and even in theoretical physics and mathematics at the turn of the century. It might be seen to be an expression of the movement of European formalism in general terms—a formalism that aims to abstract form from all questions of content and, scientifically speaking, to arrive at a complete formalization or axiomatization of any system, whether it be mathematical, physical, biological, or linguistic.

A POSTSTRUCTURALIST MARX?

In view of these developments, Carver argues that we must continually reassess Marx, and that such reassessments will change both as the political contexts change and as political theory refines and alters its methodology. He suggests that Marx will always be part of the canon either as a positive or negative point of departure, and that, with the collapse of the Soviet empire and the East/West construction of the globe, Marx should no longer be read as the theorist of the proletarian revolution but rather as "the premier theorist of commercial society." He suggests three main ways in which this reassessment of Marx is taking place today: first, a shift in *what* Marx is read; second, a shift in *how* Marx is read, and; third, a shift in *why* Marx is read. Under the first shift, Carver suggests that the traditional order of Marxian texts is not the only possible one. As new texts have been discovered, the doctrinal reasons for ordering the Marxian archive in a particular sequence have collapsed. In his account, Carver suggests: "Marx's critical work on contemporary democratic and authoritarian movements takes centre stage, along with his critique of the categories of contemporary economic life" (1998: 2).

Under the second shift, Carver argues that recent philosophical approaches and methodological refinements—Gadamer and Ricoeur's hermeneutics, Derrida's deconstruction, Cambridge contextualism—have changed once and for all how reading should be conceived, questioning the underlying humanist categories of author and writer, the notion of intention and its role in interpreting a work, and the status and functions of language itself. He suggests in this regard: "Interpretative work on Marx needs to catch up with the postmodern intellectual age" (1998: 2).

Carver advises, under the third shift, that Marx has been read as "a revolutionary, a scientist, a philosopher, an economist," but that he reads Marx as a *politician* able to make timely interventions into left-liberal politics surrounding free market/mixed economy debates and, we would add, debates around the neoliberal construction of globalization as a form of world economic integration based upon the logic of "free trade."

It is true enough that Marx's predictions of an imminent communist revolution in Europe did not come to pass. For some this is itself proof that his theories were worthless. But a renewal of Marx today ought not to depend upon the veracity and accuracy of his various predictions in a positivist scientific mode—a kind of "verificationist Marx"—but rather, more complexly, upon the adoption and development of new reading practices that can analyze Marx's guiding metaphors, clarify and experiment with the concepts Marx used and invented, identify his many authorial voices and their intonations, and, finally, reinterpret Marx's readings of other philosophers, not least, Hegel and Feuerbach.

For Carver, like Fredric Jameson, it should be easy to hold onto historical materialism as the thesis that meaning is determined by the economic, historical, material, and social circumstances of the era in which the work was produced. Jameson (1991, 1998), in a highly influential interpretation of postmodernism as "the culture of late capitalism," regards it as a mere intensification of the culture industry first noted by Horkheimer and Adorno. Yet Jameson provides a totalizing Hegelian metanarrative that other thinkers, such as Jean-François Lyotard, find objectionable.

We can briefly pursue this point concerning new practices of reading and their application to Marx by reference to Deleuze, Derrida, and Foucault. Poststructuralist thought is often seen as "post-Marxist" or even as antagonistic to

Marxism. The reading that we are proposing here uses poststructuralist approaches to the text as a means for "rescuing" Marx, in a time when right-Hegelians have proclaimed that capitalism has won and that, therefore, Marxism is dead. Poststructuralist reading practices allow us to contemplate a fluid rereading of Marx. Gilles Deleuze demonstrated his approach to the text by emphasizing *extra-textual* practices. As he wrote:

A text for me, is only a little wheel in an extra-textual practice. It is not a question of commenting on the text by a method of deconstruction, or by a method of textual practice, or by any other method; it is a question of seeing what use a text is in the extra-textual practice that prolongs the text. (Deleuze, 1973: 186–7)

In an interview with Toni Negri in 1990, Deleuze (1995: 171) maintained that both he and Guattari had remained Marxists, and he suggested that political philosophy today must be judged on its analysis of capitalism and its internal developments. He regarded as central Marx's notion that capitalism is an immanent system that constantly overcomes its own limitations. Deleuze not only suggested that he had remained a Marxist; he was working on a book called *Grandeur de Marx* at the time of his suicide.

Deleuze's reading of Marx took place at the point where Deleuze moved "from an interpretation of Nietzsche to an experiment with Nietzsche" (Schrift, 1995: 62). Peters (1996) has previously referred to Deleuze's Nietzschean critique of the Hegelian dialectic as one of the major keys to understanding French poststructuralism. Deleuze makes double use of Nietzsche's will to power. It permits Deleuze to appropriate not only the formal structure of Nietzsche's will to power but also its "content" by offering an account of both "will" and "power":

While French thought in general has worked for the past thirty years under the aegis of the three so-called "masters of suspicion" Nietzsche, Marx and Freud, we can understand Deleuze privileging Nietzsche over Marx and Freud on precisely this point. Marx operates primarily with the register of power and Freud operates primarily within the register of desire. Yet each appears blind to the overlapping of these two registers, and when they do relate them, one is clearly subordinate to the other. Nietzsche's will to power, on the other hand, makes impossible any privileging of one over the other, and his thinking functions in terms of an inclusive conjunction of desire and power. (Schrift, 1995: 68)

We might say that, equipped with these understandings, Deleuze and Guattari embark upon a Marxist form of the analysis of capitalism, which might be termed *libidinal materialism*.

In an early text originally published in 1972, Derrida talks of his relation to Marx. He suggests that his work can be described as "critique of idealism," and to that extent it is at least in sympathy with Marxism, but the theoretical elaboration between the two economies is *still to come* (1981: 62). He argues that Marx's texts (and those of the rest of the canon of Marxism) should not be regarded as "finished elaborations" that are simply to be applied: "These texts are not to be read according to a hermeneutical or exegetical method which would seek out a finished signified beneath a textual surface. Reading is transformational. . . . But this transformation cannot be executed however one wishes. It requires protocols of reading" (Derrida, 1981: 63). Derrida returns to Marx in a lecture given in 1993 in two sessions at the University of California, Riverside, at an international colloquium organized under the title of "Whither Marxism?" by Bernd Magnus and Stephen Cullenberg. That lecture, augmented and clarified, became *Specters of Marx* (Derrida, 1994). In answer to the question Derrida responds:

> It will always be a fault not to read and reread and discuss Marx . . . and to go beyond scholarly "reading" or "discussion." It will be more and more a fault, a failing of theoretical, philosophical, political responsibility. When the dogma machine and the "Marxist" ideological apparatuses . . . are in the process of disappearing, we no longer have any excuse, only alibis, for turning away from this responsibility. There will be no future without this. Not without Marx, no future without Marx, without the memory and the inheritance of Marx: in any case of a certain Marx, of his genius, of at least one of his spirits. For this will be our hypothesis or rather our bias: there is more than one of them, there must be more than one of them. (1994: 13)

Derrida's "answer" here is to keep alive the critical spirit of Marxism as a political project (the critique of capitalism, challenges to hegemonic ideologies, the valorization of labor and human freedom), while not committing himself to any orthodoxy or the logic of historical inevitability that underlies Marxism.

Similarly, Foucault wrote: "Marx is not just the author of the *Communist Manifesto* or *Das Kapital*: [he has] established an endless possibility of discourse" (1984: 114). Foucault's relation to Marxism was complex and changing. For Foucault (1991: 104), Marx, like Freud, was a "founder of discursivity" rather than a founder of a science—though, admittedly, this was not the way in which Marx saw himself. Alan Schrift tries to reconcile this tension as follows: "This is to say, their works are not corrected, but applied; they become incorporated into the ongoing discourse while at the same time remaining an object of study and a source of inspiration separate from the discursive transformation in which they participate" (1995: 34).

In other words, Foucault was not interested in the problem of how political economy as a science arose per se but rather in charting those common elements that existed among the three distinct fields of natural history, grammar, and political economy, and how they were constituted in terms of their rules during the seventeenth century and the analogous transformations they underwent during the next century. Foucault was interested in the problem of "how . . . a type of knowledge with pretenses to scientificity arise from a real practice," and this demanded a comparative analysis of "procedures internal to scientific discourse" (Foucault, 1991: 102). Foucault went on to say that he did not find the theoretical opposition between the state and civil society of traditional political theory very helpful; and that he was more interested in how a particular kind of power is exercised and manifested (1991: 164). He argued:

> We live in a social universe in which the formation, circulation, and utilization of knowledge present a fundamental problem. If the accumulation of capital has been an essential feature of our society, the accumulation of knowledge has not been any less so. Now, the exercise, production, and accumulation of this knowledge cannot be dissociated from the mechanisms of power; complex relations exist which must be analysed. (1991:165)

These reflections on poststructuralism and Marx are meant to indicate that, contrary to conventional characterizations, poststructuralism is in no way politically aloof or morally agnostic. But it is typical of their skeptical relation to overarching theory to find poststructuralists invoking and questioning some of the key concepts of Marxism—rereading Marx through a more Nietzschean than Hegelian lens. In the context of poststructuralist work in education, we will see a similarly ambivalent invocation of theory.

POSTMODERN OR POSTSTRUCTURALIST FREIRE?

There are at least two ways in which we might approach the question of Freire in relation to postmodernism and poststructuralism: One is to develop a postmodern critique of his position; another is to investigate "postmodern tendencies" in his work while still acknowledging his modernist theoretical leanings.

The first point can be developed in relation to the question of postmodernity. Habermas thinks that if modernity has failed it is because it has allowed the totality of life to become splintered into independent specialities that are now the province of experts; he looks to the arts to integrate cognitive, ethical, and political discourses, opening up the prospect of a unity of experience. We think that Freire (at least, the Freire of *Pedagogy of the Oppressed*) would side with Habermas on this question: That is to say, Freire embraced a view of culture as a totality and he based his hope for emancipation upon it. Lyotard, however, wishes to question the sort of unity Habermas has in mind. He questions the aim of Habermas's project of modernity in the constitution of a sociocultural unity, integrating cognition, ethics, and politics, and asks whether such cultural integration or synthesis is desirable or even, indeed, possible (Lyotard, 1984: 73).

Insofar as Freire situates himself in the Hegelian tradition and bases his work on the Hegelian dialectic, he is open to the same sorts of criticisms. Freire assumes the operative power and integrity of the Hegelian dialectic as the underlying principle of society. It drives his philosophy of history and provides the oppositional logic of struggle that he notes between "the oppressor" and "the oppressed." It characterizes his unitary notion of the subject, his account of political agency, and the key ontological process of *becoming* (more fully human) through education and political praxis. A Hegelian phenomenology also underlies Freire's understanding of self (and culture) as the negation of the other. One might even argue that Freire's view of language itself, of reading, writing, and "speaking the true word," is invested with the binary oppositions that typify Hegelian theory. While Freire's debt to Hegel is most evident in *Pedagogy of the Oppressed*, he makes reference to the influence of Hegel's phenomenology and dialectic in a number of other places. In Freire and Shor, for instance, he writes: "The more I approach critically the object of my observation, the more I am able to perceive that the object of my observation is not yet because it is becoming" (1987: 82). In an interview with Carlos Alberto Torres, whom Freire describes as "a man who thinks dialectically and doesn't merely talk of dialectics," Freire gives an example of this orientation toward engaging social problems:

> Today I live the enormous joy of perceiving with every passing day that the strength of education resides precisely in its limitations. The efficiency of education resides in the impossibility of doing everything. The limits of education would bring a naïve man or woman to desperation. A dialectical man or woman discovers in the limits of education the raison d'etre for his or her efficiency. It is in this way that I feel that today I am an efficient Secretary of Education because I am limited. (Torres and Freire, 1994: 106)

This situates poststructuralists in an awkward relation to Freire's educational politics and pedagogy. As we have seen, one of the distinguishing elements of French poststructuralism is precisely its Nietzsche-inspired attack on the Hegelian dialectic. As one of us has argued elsewhere (Peters, 1996, 1997), Gilles Deleuze's *Nietzsche and Philosophy*, originally published in 1962, represents one of the inaugurating moments of French poststructuralism:

> Three ideas define the dialectic: the idea of a power of the negative as a theoretical principle manifested in opposition and contradiction; the idea that suffering and sadness have value, the valorization of the "sad passions," as a practical principle manifested in splitting and tearing apart; the idea of positivity as a theoretical principle and practical product of negation itself. It is no exaggeration to say that the whole of Nietzsche's philosophy, in its polemic sense, is the attack on these three ideas. (Deleuze, 1983: 195–6)

The major French poststructuralists, Deleuze, Derrida, Foucault, and Lyotard (among others), want to contrast the negative and purely reactive power of the dialectic with the purely positive power of the affirmative inherent in "difference" as the basis for a radical thought that is neither Hegelian nor Marxist. The notion of difference in its various manifestations and formulations— *différance* (Derrida), the *differend* (Lyotard), a conjunctive *serialization* and *multiplicity* (Foucault)—is pitted against the totalizing and exhaustive synthesizing power of the Hegelian dialectic, considered as the sole metaphysical and logical principle underlying self, culture, and world history.

Lyotard, in a now-famous passage, defines "postmodern" as "incredulity towards metanarratives" (1984: xxiv), in contrast to the term "modern," which he uses "to designate any science that legitimates itself with reference to a metadiscourse of this kind making an explicit appeal to some grand narrative, such as the dialectics of the Spirit, the hermeneutics of meaning, the emancipation of the rational or working subject, or the creation of wealth" (1984: xxiii). The object of Lyotard's study is the condition of knowledge in the most highly developed societies, and his theoretical innovation is to rescue the narrative genre as a form of knowledge and apply the fruits of narratology to the question of the legitimation of knowledge and education in advanced liberal societies. Immediately, one can note crucial differences between Lyotard and Freire: Where Lyotard focuses upon the bankruptcy of Enlightenment metanarratives as no longer providing a successful legitimation for knowledge in advanced capitalist societies because knowledge has become fully commodified, Freire is concerned with the prospect of emancipation effected through mass literacy programs in the Third World context. Their respective theoretical and geopolitical orientations could not be more different.

Yet even given these differences there are "postmodern tendencies" in Freire's work: his emphasis on the text and text analogues for understanding the world; his emphasis upon subjectivity, experience, and culture; and, to some extent, his understanding of oppression and the exercise of power. Freire, toward the end of his life, began to address the way in which his work could be brought into play with certain aspects of postmodern and poststructuralist thought. Indeed, it could be argued that Freire began to revise his earlier humanist Marxist ideas by reference to critical postmodern social theory. Some theorists who have worked in close collaboration with Freire on this project include Henry Giroux, Peter McLaren, Tomaz Tadeu da Silva, and bell hooks (see the essays in McLaren and Leonard, 1993). Other Freire scholars, such as Peter Roberts (1996), have also proposed readings of Freire in relation to postmodernism. McLaren and Lankshear (1993) put forward a view of critical literacy that is decidedly postmodern, but argue that decentering the subject and the text represent obstacles to postmodern social theory from within. Roberts provides a representation of *conscientization* that is linked to the ideal of praxis and more sensitive to recent criticisms of universalist thought and subject-centered reason. He reinterprets *conscientization* in light of the postmodernist notion of multiple subjectivities.

At the same time, it is important to note that Freire was wary of "postmodernism" and, while agreeing with Giroux and McLaren, he warns about how "excursions into the discourse of postmodern social theory are often purchased at the price of sacrificing narratives of freedom underwritten by an ethical imagination" (cited in McLaren and Leonard, 1993: x). Clearly, Freire passed through different phases over the long history of his work, reflecting different influences upon him. We posit three phases: an early liberal phase driven by the concerns of liberation theology; a more clearly recognizable Marxist or neo-Marxist phase, imbued with a phenomenological/existential humanism; and finally, perhaps, a more postmodern phase, where he was prepared to entertain the claims of a critical (rather than conservative) postmodern social theory where these claims gelled with or helped to recast aspects of his own work.

For instance, Freire addressed the question of postmodern tendencies in his own work when he suggested that "it is important to appreciate the multiplicity of modes of oppression. . . . [I]t is equally important to discount claims to a unitary experience of oppression. . . . Oppression must be understood in its multiple and contradictory instances . . . without resorting to transcendental guarantees" (qtd. in McLaren and Leonard, 1993: x). He said that he always challenged the essentialism underlying claims of a unitary experience. Addressing himself squarely to the question of democracy and liberation, he wrote:

> A way to avoid both the totalizing Eurocentric and androcentric logic with its Hegelian roots, and the pessimism that comes from a critical theory solely trapped within a philosophy of non-identity. . . . Postmodern theorists have begun to make clear in their writings that what must contingently ground identity in a postmodern world in which subjectivity has become unmoored from its former narratives of social justice is a postcolonial politics of ethics and compassion. (Freire, 1993: xii)

Freire's acknowledgment and treatment of postmodern social theory here was not an isolated occurrence. In *Pedagogy of Hope*, Freire he said that he wanted to "explain and defend progressive postmodernity" and "reject conservative, neoliberal postmodernity" (1994: 10). Against the old-fashioned sectarianism of the Left (and the easy accommodations of the Right) he proclaimed: "Let us be postmodern: radical and utopian. Progressive" (1994: 51). He referred to "the crumbling away of the authoritarian socialist world" and said he wanted to purge the old socialist Left of "its authoritarian distortions, its totalitarian repulsiveness, its sectarian blindness" (1994: 96). Specifically, Freire wanted to rid Marxism of its authoritarianism and its lack of tolerance of diversity and difference: "What is becoming needful, among other things, is that Marxists get over their smug certainty that they are modern, adopt an attitude of humility in dealing with the popular classes, and become postmodernly less smug and less certain—progressively postmodern" (1994: 96). Freire made much of this distinction, contrasting a dogmatic, intolerant, and reactionary Marxism with a critical, reflective, and tolerant version, and returned to it frequently, especially in his later books and, in particular, in his work on higher education.

Yet for all his modulation of his earlier work with the themes of postmodernism, Freire did not believe that classes had disappeared, or that, under neoliberalism, inequalities had not widened, or that gender and race did not cut across and intersect these inequalities in complex ways. For Freire, these remained clear, objective truths. In *Pedagogy of the City*, he refers to his utopian dream in the following way: "My love for reading and writing . . . has to do with the creation of a society that is less perverse, less discriminatory, less racist, less *machista* than the society we now have" (1993: 140). What he bequeathed to us is an unfailing commitment to questions of social justice, a demand for participatory democracy in a fuller, deeper sense, and a critical stance toward literacy and pedagogy. This legacy, along with the rereadings of Marx mentioned earlier, continues to exercise a powerful influence upon educational research from poststructural scholars as well as others.

THREE EXEMPLARS OF POSTSTRUCTURALIST RESEARCHERS IN EDUCATION

As we have tried to make clear, it is a mistake to identify poststructuralism—a decidedly ambiguous and increasingly homogenizing label for a complex intellectual movement—with one set of philosophers, one set of doctrines, or one set of research "methods." By focusing upon the work of three prominent researchers in the field of education (and related disciplines) we mean simply to identify three exemplars who have undertaken significant work in the field of education by making use of insights from poststructuralism and by adopting aspects of poststructuralist thinking or modes of analysis. But these researchers are as significant in their differences as in their commonalities. In singling out the work of Henry Giroux, Patti Lather, and Stephen Ball, we do not mean to imply that they are part of a unified "poststructuralist" camp. Indeed, all three exhibit strong differences and their "projects" must be distinguished from one another. Indeed, their differences are among the reasons we have chosen them. Nor do we mean to suggest that these are the best or the only scholars working in this area. We could just as well have chosen to focus on the work of Thomas Popkewitz, Cleo Cherryholmes, James Marshall, Peter McLaren, Paul Smeyers, Elizabeth Ellsworth, Colin Lankshear, Paul Standish, Alison Jones, Bill Green, Richard Smith, Megan Boler, Richard Edwards, Tina Besley, Peter Roberts, John Fritzman, Tuan Nuyen, Carol Nicholson, Pradeep Dhillon, Nigel Blake, Bernadette Baker, Wanda Pillow, or any one of a number of exciting younger scholars who are adopting, modifying, and developing poststructuralist modes of analysis.

Henry Giroux: Critical Pedagogy, Popular Culture, and Postmodernism

If there is one thing that separates critical pedagogy—the specifically American strand exemplified best by Henry Giroux—from critical theory, especially the founding fathers, Max Horkheimer and Theodor Adorno, it is the attitude toward popular culture and the position of intellectuals within it. In their classic essay "The Culture Industry," Horkheimer and Adorno (1972) argue that the same logic of commodification evident in the sphere of production organizes the sphere of consumption: The instrumental rationality of exchange-value obliterates all cultural difference and tradition, reducing everything to the same universal scale of monetary value. In their analysis of the culture of capitalist modernity, one detects a distinctive European cultural pessimism evidenced in the general intellectual mood of Continental nihilism following the outbreak of two world wars, as well as a nostalgia for an organic cultural unity—a time when manifestations of "high" culture were unified and given some metaphysical justification under a ruling metanarrative.

By contrast, one finds neither pessimism nor nostalgia in the recent works of Henry Giroux. His attitude is the attitude of the "New World" intellectual, distinctly American, utopian, and built upon an awareness of the ways in which cultures are *made*: Giroux's attitude is imbued with a critical spirit, sharing an emancipatory impulse with critical theory, yet it is fiercely anti-elitist and approaches popular culture, and especially youth culture, in more "democratic" ways. We see these attitudes expressed by Giroux in the preface of *Disturbing Pleasures: Learning Popular Culture*, where he speaks of his own experience growing up in a working-class neighborhood and the peculiar tension between popular culture and schooling:

> Popular culture was where the action was—it marked out a territory where pleasure, knowledge, and desire circulated in close proximity to the life of the streets. There was always something forbidden about this culture, with its comics, pinball machines, restricted codes, visual excesses, and overly masculine orientation. . . . We felt rather than knew what was really useful knowledge. And we talked, danced, and lost ourselves in a street culture that never stopped moving. Then we went to school. (1991 ix)

School was a different planet, Giroux remarks, "exclusively centered on obscure books and the culture of print" and "oriented toward a cheap imitation of the knowledge of high culture" (1991: ix). Giroux remarks that while he was force-fed Latin, Western civilization, math, spelling, and the like, and sold the meritocratic myth that success at school was the only passport to middle class opportunity, the fact was that his identity was largely fashioned outside of school. As he says: "Films, books, journals, videos, and music in different and significant ways did more to shape my politics and life than did my formal education, which always seemed about somebody else's dreams" (1991: x).

Giroux, perhaps more than any contemporary theorist in education other than Freire, has argued for a pedagogy that involves the creation of a new kind of public sphere; Giroux has sought to protect and enlarge that sphere by reexamining popular culture and the way that "the pedagogical and the political come together in sites that are often ignored by the school." In these sites, "the struggle over knowledge, power and authority translates itself into a broader battle over the meaning of pleasure, self-formation, and national identity" (1991: x). Giroux's pedagogical innovations and recommendations grow out of and demonstrate a commitment to the developing tradition of critical pedagogy based upon, but in many respects going beyond, the work of Freire.

Giroux constitutes one of the "new intellectuals" in the sense described by Andrew Ross when he suggested that intellectuals today will be guided by "the pragmatic, democratizing possibilities ushered in by the new technologies and new popular cultures in a hegemonic capitalist society." Such intellectuals are unlikely to understand the new politics of knowledge if they do not recognize why so many cultural forms "draw their popular appeal from expressions of disrespect for the lessons of educated taste" (Ross, 1990: 237). Hence, Ross emphasizes that if intellectuals today have any role to play it is in relation to popular culture; their role is informed by the same matrix of power and desire experienced by other consumers, and their task is to begin to rearticulate the popular in ways that confront its worst excesses. To this degree, then, he not only accepts the "postmodern" collapse of the distinction between high culture and popular culture, but he firmly locates the new intellectual's primary critical role in relation to forms of popular culture. Similarly, S. Hall considers the new interest in culture "an attempt to address the manifest break-up of traditional culture," especially traditional class cultures (1990: 12). The notion of "culture" has become more anthropologically differentiated and its newly understood complexity has been instrumental in helping initiate and delineate cultural studies as a field of legitimate academic interest (see Johnson, 1986; Hall, 1990; Peters, 1996).

Giroux has taken a similar "turn" to cultural studies and now operates as an interpreter or "cultural hermeneuticist" in the postmodern age, as opposed to a legislator in the modern age (Bauman, 1987). In face of a wider rationalization of society and consumer-driven culture, which have fragmented traditional forms of cultural authority and left the market as the only link between subsystems, the task of intellectuals as interpreters has become to critique the dominant modes of social integration, including "education" in the widest sense of not only schooling, but neighborhoods, media, and popular culture. Thus, Giroux (1991) analyzes promotional culture in the postmodern age, considering, as an example, the shift in Benetton's advertising strategy from 1984 to 1991. He offers this analysis as part of a wider politics and pedagogy of representation and argues for the need to develop critical public cultures. He also examines "the wonderful world of Disney," analyzing the link in Disney films between issues of memory, politics, and identity, and the way in which big business has redefined the purpose and meaning of public schooling in the Reagan/Bush era.

In a chapter entitled "The Turn Toward Theory," Giroux (1991) addresses "the importance of appropriating selective aspects of literary theory and poststructuralism as part of the broader attempt to develop an insurgent pedagogy/ies aimed at reconstructing and animating numerous critical public cultures" (1991: 110). Giroux's understanding of poststructuralism is insightful; he reviews the easy dismissal and nondialectical engagement with poststructuralism offered by educational theorists of more traditionally Marxist and liberal persuasions. His conclusion is that poststructuralism in the service of critical pedagogy focuses upon one of the central issues in education: "The need for a better conception of the relationship between agency and subjectivity" (1991: 122).

Elsewhere, Aronowitz and Giroux suggest that "emancipatory postmodernism" shares with modernism a critical, reflexive approach to knowledge that challenges foundational metanarratives and contests right-wing appropriations of postmodernism (1991: 19). For these authors empowerment is still the bottom line. In the chapter "Postmodernism and the Discourse of Educational Criticism," Aronowitz and Giroux reinterpret educational research in terms of the model of criticism and frame the question of postmodern education by reference to a threefold crisis of modernism: the crisis of totality and foundationalism; the crisis of cultural authority and the problematic of Otherness; and the crisis of language, presentation, and agency. The first crisis refers to the wholesale intellectual attack against all forms of foundationalist epistemology, including the critique of positivism and neopositivism, as well as the rejection of totalizing metanarratives. The second crisis is the breakdown of a sharp distinction between traditional and popular culture, with the added argument that stresses "the importance of minority cultures as historically specific forms of cultural production" (1991: 70). The third crisis refers to "the importance of language and subjectivity as new fronts from which to rethink the issues of meaning, identity, and politics" (1991: 75). This represents a useful formulation of the importance of postmodernism and poststructuralism to educational research and theory.

Giroux's work is located at the forefront of recent theoretical debates in social and educational theory and cultural criticism. He extends the parameters of critical pedagogy, revising or perhaps reinventing Paulo Freire's dictum of the word-world relation by relocating critical methods and strategies for "reading" and "writing" outside the classroom and into the world of popular culture. By doing so he crystallizes a distinctively "American" left-wing approach to questions of culture, implicitly distinguishing himself from the first generation of critical theorists.

Patti Lather: Poststructuralist Feminist Praxis in Education

In this section we briefly review Patti Lather's (1991) *Getting Smart* as an exemplar of feminist research in education that attempts to develop a critical approach to pedagogy informed by poststructuralism. In the introduction, series editor Michael Apple nicely sets the tone in the following passage: "The form postmodernism takes is that of the self-conscious, self-contradictory, self-undermining statement. It wants to provide a thoroughgoing 'denaturizing' critique, to 'detoxify' our cultural representations and to show their political importance" (1991: vii). Lather herself states the three aims of her book clearly:

> (1) to mark the development of what philosopher of science Brian Fay (1987) terms "a critical social science" in what is more generally referred to as "the postpositivist climate of our times" . . . ; (2) to contribute to the theory and practice of liberatory education; and (3) to explore the implications of feminism, neo-Marxism and poststructuralism for developing inquiry-approaches in the human sciences that move us forward toward ways of knowing which interrupt relations of dominance and subordination. (xvii)

Each of these three aims, she suggests, is grounded in "getting smart" about the conditions under which we live.

Lather views these theoretical trends in close relation to each other. For example, she focuses on how poststructuralism encourages feminist researchers to examine "otherness" and to make this trope central to their reflections on their research. It is a lesson that Lather first applies to herself: "As a first-world woman—white, middle-class, North American, heterosexual—my self-described positionality shifts from 'post-Marxist feminist' to 'postmodern materialist-feminist'" (1991: xix). This sort of self-reflexivity is given greater emphasis here than in most methodologies and it is indebted to poststructuralist thought, especially to "new French feminisms," including the work of Cixous, Kristeva, and Irigaray, for nuanced accounts of subjectivity in relation to questions of subordination and resistance.

Lather's book is an early attempt not only to draw from poststructuralist thought in order to do research in a postpositivist climate, but also to write in a "postmodern" way, as she puts it, "to simultaneously use and call into question a discourse, to both challenge and inscribe dominant meaning systems in ways that construct our own categories and frameworks as contingent, positioned, partial" (1991: 1). Lather spells out some of the other assumptions that guide her work: the failure of positivism (its inability to provide a theoretical justification of its own endeavors); the value-ladenness of inquiry (and the inherently perspectival, culture-bound ways of knowing); the possibilities of critical social science (with its critique of instrumental reason); the politics of empowerment (which demands that social science be empowering); and, the challenges of postmodernism (which challenges a modernist politics of emancipation) (1991: 1–4).

At the heart of her project is the notion of "getting smart"—the question of a postmodern praxis that is, at once, open-ended in terms of the struggle over truth and reality, nonfoundational in epistemology, not prescribed by an historical telos, self-reflexive and willfully undermining of our interpretive frames, and yet still oriented toward resistance and committed to social change:

> Postmodernism offers feminists ways to work within and yet challenge dominant discourses. Within postmodernist feminism, language moves from representational to constitutive; binary logic implodes, and debates about "the real" shift from a radical constructivism to a discursively reflexive position which recognizes how our knowledge is mediated by the concepts and categories of our understanding. Hegemonic forms of academic discourse are thoroughly challenged, including those at play in our intendedly counter-hegemonic work. . . . [P]ostmodernism offers feminism opportunities to avoid dogmatism and the reductionism of single-cause analysis, to produce knowledge from which to act, and to diffuse power as a means to take advantage of the range of mobile and transitory points of resistance inherent in the networks of power relations. (1991: 39)

Lather then proceeds to list what she calls the negatives of postmodernism, including: the priority of aesthetics over ethics; an emphasis on language that forgets traditional questions concerning the maldistribution of global resources and power; the ways in which complex cultural differences become easily packaged ("too often, positively valued marginality deteriorates into first-world appropriation of third-world difference," p. 40); the lack of an effective theory of agency, which tends to deny the possibility of collective action; and, finally, the inaccessibility of the discourse itself, which is often intended for small and very specialized academic audiences.

Lather's work is important not only in its trail-blazing notion of "research as praxis" and in reviewing feminist research approaches to empowering methodologies, but also in clarifying the stakes of emancipatory education. (Research-as-praxis is a notion of research built on the collapse of theory and practice: Research is not conceived as the application of theory, but rather emerges out of reflection on practice in an ongoing process). Lather usefully explores the relations between the discourses of postmodernism and emancipatory education by reference to Ellsworth's essay "Why Doesn't This Feel Empowering?" (which criticizes, among others, Henry Giroux and other Freireans). Ellsworth argues

> Examining the discourses within which critical pedagogues are caught up, the concepts of empowerment, student voice, dialogue and the term "critical" itself are problematized by asking "which interpretations and 'sense making' do these discourses facilitate, which do they silence and marginalize, and what interests do they appear to serve?" (Ellsworth 1989: 298)

Basically, Lather reviews Ellsworth's interrogation of critical pedagogy's rationalism and the "violence of rationalism against its Others" (cited in Lather, 1991: 43). The problem that this introduces is nicely expressed in the following remark from Lather: "How can . . . self-reflexivity both render our basic assumptions problematic and provisional and yet still propel us to take a stand?"(1991: 44). If postmodernism "destabilizes assumptions of interpretive validity," then in the "post-critical position" what reasons do we have for taking a political or ethical stand? Lather's answer to this important and vexing question is given in the following passage: "Ellsworth's project can be read as an example of how deconstruction can serve to problematize critical pedagogy in ways that resituate our emancipatory work as opposed to destroy it" (1991: 47).

Lather's important work has built upon, and contributed to, a broader body of work conducted by feminists such as Linda Alcoff, Linda Nicholason, Susan Bordo, Deborah Britzman, Donna Haraway, Sandra Harding, Jane Flax, Nancy Fraser, Elizabeth Grosz, Meaghan Morris, Gayatri Spivak, and many others. In the field of educational studies, feminist poststructuralist theory and method has become quickly established as an influential research orientation (see St. Pierre and Pillow, 2000).

Stephen Ball: Foucault, Critical Ethnography, and Educational Policy Studies

Stephen Ball provides an approach to educational policy studies that combines ethnography and aspects of poststructuralist thinking to study the micro-politics of schools and the impact of recent educational reform in the United Kingdom. In his early edited collection, *Foucault and Education: Disciplines and Knowledge* (1990), Ball focuses upon Foucault's work on the human sciences in relation to processes of normalization in education and the establishment of educational sites "as generators of an historically specific (modern) discourse" (1990: 3) that carry with them the right and authority to speak. Ball recounts the impetus behind Foucault's history as one that investigates the development of different modes by which human beings are made subjects; to this end he recalls Foucault's notion of "dividing practices" as those practices involving the objectification of the subject through processes of classification. Dividing practices, he notes, are central "to the organizational processes of education in our society":

> The testing, examining, profiling, and streaming in education, the use of entry criteria for different types of schooling, and the formation of different types of intelligence, ability, and scholastic ability in the processes of schooling are all examples of such "dividing practices." In these ways, using these techniques and forms of organization, and the creation of separate and different curricula, pedagogies, forms of teacher-student relationships, identities and subjectivities are formed, learned and carried. (1990: 4)

As he goes on to remark, these dividing practices are part of the formation of a burgeoning and ever more sophisticated network of educational sciences, practices, and technologies harnessed to produce the "truth" about and address the educational problems of the day, whether these be defined as "inequality," "underachievement," or "cultural deprivation." Hence, like other theorists described here, Ball wants to critically explore issues of educational research methodology in terms of how they operate within a power/knowledge system: How research categories and constructs, for example, also play a central role in the formation of human subjects, institutional practices, and technologies of control that discipline and normalize the identities available to actors in schools.

Not surprisingly, Ball's collection focuses strongly on *Discipline and Punish* in that Ball articulates and elaborates Foucault's power/knowledge formulation and suggests that education during the nineteenth and twentieth centuries is an indispensable part of a Foucauldian analysis of society, not only in relation to the development of credentialism as the basis for modern society but also in terms of the growth of a group of experts and intellectuals associated with education. Ball suggests that education is especially ripe for a Foucauldian analysis because education, in the formal sense of mass institutions, "works not only to render its students as subjects of power, it also constitutes them, or some of them, as powerful agents" (1990: 5).

In his later work, Ball brings together elements of an approach that uses Foucault to marry critical ethnography and educational policy studies. He undertakes the challenge of unifying these theories and approaches to "straddle somewhat uncomfortably, a crucial epistemological divide, in trying to marry and use the different perspectives" (Ball, 1994: 43). He clearly wants to be actively engaged in real world issues (1994: 171). His *Beachside Comprehensive: A Case-study of Secondary Schooling* is a traditional ethnography, yet even here he is a little apprehensive about the "scientific" nature of the process: Participant observation was "based upon convenience and availability" (1981: 25) and he suggests that he did not enter "into my field of study with specific hypotheses to test or a rigidly predetermined research design" (1981: 280). Later, he defines ethnography as

> a way of engaging critically with, and developing interpretations of the real . . . it is disruptive, it is often about giving voice to the unheard, it is also about the play of power-knowledge relations in local and specific settings; here, the curriculum, management, leadership, choice and competition. It enables the analyst to focus and explore "events," spaces which divide those in struggle. (Ball 1994: 4)

While Ball maintains an ambivalence about certain versions of poststructuralism he consistently emphasizes the critical element of poststructuralism, especially in relation to Foucault's thinking and the method of genealogy. He is intent upon "unmasking the politics that underlie some of the apparent neutrality of educational reform" (Ball 1990: 7). Genealogy as a form of critique releases "the diverse voices of marginalized or oppressed social groups as well as accessing the voices of authority and influence" (Ball, 1994: 4). He suggests that "educational ethnography has been oriented to the exploration and documentation of resistance and the interplay of dominations and struggle" (Ball, 1994: 4). While advocating the marriage of different theories and approaches he readily admits the difficulties he faces as a researcher: "I am certainly ready to confess to contradiction. I continue to hold and want to juggle with and attempt to integrate a set of disparate epistemological and theoretical positions . . . in this sense I am no purist" (Ball, 1994: 171). This ambivalent, self-critical stance echoes the position of Lather.

One of the major distinguishing elements of Ball's critical ethnography is its difference from traditional Marxist theories and Marxist-informed ethnographies. This is seen most clearly in Ball's view of the state and its influence in making policy. As he writes, "Class relations, sectional interests are represented in policy and exercise influence upon the State. It is neither autonomous nor independent. In particular, its independence is governed by capital accumulation" (1990: 20). Yet, he maintains, "the State is a site of conflict and incoherence" (1990: 21) and "The State cannot have intentions unless these are expressed in terms of social mechanisms" (1990: 19). In other words, he says, "I do not see the State as committee acting upon the interest of the bourgeoisie. I do not accept that the problem of capital accumulation and the maintenance of its condition provide the major problem and interest effect in the working of the State" (1994: 4).

Ball's criticism of many neo-Marxists is that they neglect to analyze the relationship between economy and the state as an *empirical* question; traditionally, Marxists see a relatively instrumental link—that the state must react in ways that serve to promote the maximization of capital (at least overall and in the long run, if not in every instance). But this a priori, necessary linkage denies history and any part that it might play in influencing events in the present. On the traditional Marxist account we are doomed to repeat history (1994: 178). As he argues: "My point is that if our analyses remain concentrated entirely upon the coercive State-centered power then we run the risk of neglecting other more subtle forms of power" (1994: 178). Foucault is clearly of use to Ball in developing this more complex, less instrumental view of power. And if this more complex linkage is true of the economy and the state, it is even truer in the complicated and contradictory ways in which educational policies get formulated and implemented.

THE COMMITMENTS OF
POSTSTRUCTURALIST RESEARCHERS IN EDUCATION

It is clear that all three of these educational researchers are committed to social and political change, and explicitly see their research in this context. They conceive of their work as making a difference to their research constituents, their colleagues, and themselves. As we have sketched this story there is continuity with committed Marxist, neo-Marxist, or even left-liberal educational researchers who, along with more "scientistic" or positivistic researchers, carved up between them the study of the educational policies and practices of the welfare state. Poststructuralist researchers also share the desire to promote change for the better and to empower their constituencies. But there is more of a desire by poststructuralists to identify the plural faces of inequality and understand its dynamic and changing character, just as there is a greater willingness to understand the complex ways in which forms of oppression and disadvantage run across and through lines of class, gender, and ethnicity (as well as exhibiting other forms). There is no less of a desire to want to change those aspects of the social world that are seen as unjust, unequal, or plainly oppressive. Yet there is a more nuanced understanding of power—the multiple forms it assumes, both its dominating and productive forms, its discursive and institutional guises, and how it is exercised. And there is certainly a greater ambiguity, even unease, about reflecting upon the practices of one's own research and the choices inherent in it (such as the choice of methods, problems, and definitions), as implicated within larger power/knowledge dynamics. Informed by (we almost wrote "burdened by") such constraints, the poststructuralist educational researcher is less ready to assume the "reality" of certain social or cultural forms, the official lines of thought, the neutrality of certain methods, or the dynamics of educational research and policy in terms of a transparent, consistent, or coherent process.

Poststructuralist researchers tend to view social "reality" in terms of a mutable set of cultural practices—something complex, dynamic, and often contradictory. They also tend to recognize that this "reality" can be read in different ways and from different perspectives: In particular, poststructuralist researchers tend to emphasize structures of *desire* as much as structures of power in the ways that individuals and institutions are constituted. Poststructuralist researchers in education are drawn to new problems that tend to encourage reflection upon both the role and status of the researcher and the researched, but also upon traditional research methods themselves. For instance, the poststructuralist problematic of subjectivity and otherness generates a series of issues that require rethinking the conduct and writing of ethnography (see St. Pierre and Pillow, 2000).

More than any single development, the generation of new methods, such as deconstruction or genealogy, has meant that poststructuralist researchers in education are now challenging existing research practices and experimenting with new ways of making sense of the world. Perhaps most important, drawing upon the developments of structuralism, poststructuralist researchers in education are relearning the importance and mutability of *language*—discourses, narratives, texts, and text analogues of all kinds. These researchers have developed a new sophistication in relation to analyzing texts, discourse, and narratives, and also in relation to the activities of reading and writing themselves (including the reading and writing of research).

Finally, poststructuralist researchers are developing a better philosophical sense of what is at stake when one comes to do research, gaining a healthy skepticism for what counts as "knowledge," "education," "research," and "science," and questioning the apparent naturalness of these categories. Poststructuralism developed, in part, as a philosophical response to the scientific pretensions of both structuralism and positivism: One of the effects of this response has been to challenge researchers to reexamine themselves, their own practices, and the institution called "science."

REFERENCES

Aronowitz, S., and H. Giroux. 1991. *Postmodern Education: Politics, Culture, and Social Criticism*: Minneapolis: University of Minnesota Press.

Ball, S. J. 1981. *Beachside Comprehensive: A Case-study of Secondary Schooling*. Cambridge: Cambridge University Press.

———. 1990. *Politics and Policy-making in Education: Explorations in Policy Sociology*. New York: Routledge.

———. 1994. *Education Reform: A Critical and Post-structural Approach*. Buckingham, U.K., and Philadelphia, Pa.: Open University Press.

Bauman, Zigmunt. 1987. *Legislators and Interpreters: On Modernity, Post-modernity, and Intellectuals*. Cambridge: Polity Press, in association with B. Blackwell.

Carver, Terell. 1998. *The Postmodern Marx*. Manchester, U.K.: Manchester University Press.

Deleuze, Gilles. 1973. "Discussion" following "Pensée nomade." Pp.186–87 in *Nietzsche aujourd'hui*. Paris: Union Générale D'Éditions.

———. 1983. *Nietzsche and Philosophy*. Translated by Hugh Tomlinson. New York: Columbia University Press.

———. 1995. "Control and Becoming." In *Negotiations, 1972–1990*. Translated by M. Joughlin. New York: Columbia University Press.

Dosse. 1997. *History of Structuralism*. Vols. 1 and 2. Translated by Deborah Glassman. Minneapolis: University of Minnesota Press.

Derrida, Jacques. [1972] 1981. *Positions*. Translated by A. Bass. Chicago: University of Chicago Press.

———. 1994. *Specters of Marx: The State of Debt, the Work of Mourning, and the New International*. Translated by Peggy Kamuf with an introduction by Bernd Magnus and Stephen Cullenberg. New York: Routledge.

Eisenstadt, S. 1989. "Introduction: Culture and Social Structure in Recent Sociological Analysis." In *Social Structure and Culture*. Edited by H. Haferkamp. Berlin and New York: de Gruyter.

Ellsworth, Elizabeth. 1989. "Why Doesn't This Feel Empowering? Working through the Repressive Myths of Critical Pedagogy." *Harvard Educational Review* 59, 3: 297–324.

Fay, Brian. 1987. *Critical Social Science: Liberation and Its Limits*. Cambridge: Blackwell in assoc. with Polity.

Featherstone, M. 1989. "Towards a Sociology of Postmodern Culture." In *Social Structure and Culture*. Edited by H. Haferkamp. Berlin and New York: de Gruyter.

———. 1990. "Global Culture: An Introduction." *Theory, Culture, and Society* 7, 2–3 (June): 1–14.

Foster, H. 1985. "Postmodernism: A Preface." In *Postmodern Culture*. Edited by H. Foster. London: Pluto Press.

Foucault, Michel. 1984. "What is an Author?" Translated by Josué V. Harari. In *The Foucault Reader*. Edited by Paul Rabinow. New York: Pantheon Books.

———. 1991. *Remarks on Marx: Conversations with Duccio Trombadori*. Translated by R. Goldstein and J. Cascaito. New York: Semiotexte.

Freire, P., and I. Shor. 1987. *A Pedagogy for Liberation*. London: MacMillan.

Freire, Paulo. 1993. *Pedagogy of the City*. New York: Continuum.

Freire, Paulo. 1994. *Pedagogy of Hope: Reliving Pedagogy of the Oppressed*. Translated by Robert R. Barr with notes by Ana Maria Araújo Freire. New York: Continuum.

Giroux, H. 1991. *Disturbing Pleasures: Learning Popular Culture*. New York: Routledge.

——. 1996. *Fugitive Cultures: Race, Violence, and Youth*. New York: Routledge.

Hall, S. 1990. "Clinging to the Wreckage: A Conversation." *Marxism Today*. September: 28–31.

Horkheimer, Max, and Theodor W. Adorno. 1972. "The Culture Industry." In *Dialectic of Enlightenment*. Translated by J. Cumming. New York: Seabury Press.

Jameson, F. 1991. *Postmodernism, or, the Cultural Logic of Late Capitalism*. London: Verso.

——. 1998. *The Origins of Postmodernity*. London: Verso.

Jencks, Charles. 1996. *What Is Postmodernism?* 4th ed. London: Academy Editions.

Johnson, R. 1986. "The Story So Far: and Further Transformations." Pp. 277–313 in *Introduction to Contemporary Cultural Studies*. Edited by D. Punter. Harlow: U.K.: Longman.

Lankshear, Colin, and Peter McLaren, eds. 1993. *Critical Literacy: Politics, Praxis, and the Postmodern*. Foreword by Maxine Green. New York: State University of New York.

Lather, Patti. 1991. *Getting Smart: Feminist Research and Pedagogy with/in the Postmodern*. New York: Routledge.

Lyotard, Jean-François. 1984. *The Postmodern Condition: A Report on Knowledge*. Translated by Geoff Benninton and Brian Massumi with a foreword by Fredric Jameson. Minneapolis: University of Minnesota Press.

McLaren, Peter, and Colin Lankshear. 1993. "Critical Literacy and the Postmodern Turn." In *Critical Literacy: Politics, Praxis, and the Postmodern*. Foreword by Maxine Green. New York: State University of New York.

McLaren, Peter, and Peter Leonard. 1993. *Paulo Freire: A Critical Encounter*. Foreword by Paulo Freire. New York: Routledge.

Peters, Michael A. 1996. *Poststructuralism, Politics, and Education*. Westport, Conn., and London: Bergin and Garvey.

——. 1997. "What is Poststructuralism? The French Reception of Nietzsche." *Political Theory Newsletter* 8, 2: 39–55.

Peters, Michael A., and Colin Lankshear. 1994. "Education and Hermeneutics: A Freirean Interpretation." In *Politics of Liberation: Paths from Freire*. Edited by Peter McLaren and Colin Lankshear. New York: Routledge.

Roberts, Peter. 1996. "Rethinking Conscientisation." *Journal of Philosophy of Education* 30, 2: 179–96.

Ross, A. 1988. "Introduction." Pp. vii–xviii in *Universal Abandon? The Politics of Postmodernism*. Edited by A. Ross. Minneapolis: University of Minnesota Press.

——. 1990. *No Respect: Intellectuals and Popular Culture*. New York: Routledge.

Saussure, Ferdinand. [1916] 1959. *Course in General Linguistics.* Edited by Charles Bally and Albert Sechehaye (with Albert Reidlinger). Translated by Wade Baskin. New York: The Philosophical Library.

Schrift, Alan. 1995. *Nietzsche's French Legacy: A Genealogy of Poststructuralism.* New York: Routledge.

St. Pierre, Elizabeth, and Wanda Pillow. 2000. *Working the Ruins: Feminist Poststructural Theory and Methods in Education.* New York: Routledge.

Torres, C. A., and P. Freire. 1994. "Twenty Years after *Pedagogy of the Oppressed*: Paulo Freire in Conversation with Carlos Alberto Torres." Pp. 100–107 in *Politics of Liberation: Paths from Freire.* Edited by P. McLaren and C. Lankshear. New York: Routledge.

Index

Abrams, M. H., 10
Adorno, Theodor, 91–94
Althusser, Louis, 8, 15, 17, 60, 82
Anglo-American thought, 35–36
Annales group, 82
anthropology, 14–15
anti-essentialism, 28
anti-foundationalism, 24
Apple, Michael, 94
archaeology, Foucauldian, 59–62
Archaeology of Knowledge, The
    (Foucault), 43, 61
authority, critique of, 69–70
autonomy, personal, 38

Bachelard, Gaston, 18, 61
Bacon, Francis, 9, 21, 35, 50
Ball, Stephen, 1, 6, 64, 96–99
Barthes, Roland, 2, 8, 15, 17, 19–20, 60,
    82
Bataille, Georges, 18, 74
Baudrillard, Jean, 19
Bauman, Zygmunt, 8
Beauvoir, Simone de, 73
behaviorism, 35
Bell, Daniel, 11
Benamou, Michel, 11
Benetton, 93

Bentham, Jeremy, 46, 62
Berkeley, George, 34
Besley, Tina, 64
Beuys, Josef, 10
Bhabha, Homi, 9
binary oppositions, 5, 19, 26, 70
bio-power, 27, 46
Blanchot, Maurice, 18, 19
Broadhead, L. A., 61–62
Bush, George W., 49
Butler, Judith, 9

Canguilhem, Georges, 18, 61
Caputo, John, 72–73
Caramello, Charles, 11
Carver, Terell, 82–83
Casey, Kathleen, 57
Chanter, Tina, 75
Cherryholmes, Cleo, 55
Chomsky, Noam, 16
Cicero, Marcus Tullius, 38
Cixous, Hélène, 25, 73, 74, 95
classical studies, 38
Clifford, James, 9
Comte, August, 35
Connolly, William, 9
conscientization, 89
consciousness. *See* subject, human

About the Authors

Michael A. Peters is research professor in the Faculty of Education at the University of Glasgow. He has written extensively on the subject of post-structuralism and education including the recent book, *Poststructuralism, Politics, and Education*.

Nicholas C. Burbules is professor of educational policy studies at the University of Illinois, Urbana-Champaign, editor of the journal *Educational Theory*, author of *Dialogue in Teaching*, and coeditor of *Teaching and its Predicaments*.